THE
ENGLISH
COUNTRY
HOUSE
EXPLAINED

TREVOR YORKE

COUNTRYSIDE BOOKS
NEWBURY BERKSHIRE

First published 2012
© Trevor Yorke 2012

COUNTRYSIDE BOOKS
3 Catherine Road
Newbury, Berkshire

To view our complete range of books,
please visit us at
www.countrysidebooks.co.uk

ISBN 978 1 84674 301 6

Designed by Peter Davies, Nautilus Design
Produced through MRM Associates Ltd., Reading
Typeset by CJWT Solutions, St Helens
Printed by Information Press, Oxford

CONTENTS

Introduction

❖

The English country house is an imposing record of aristocratic wealth, innovative architecture and fashionable interior design; a glorious museum of world art and personal history bottled up in one unique building. More than this, it reflects the whims of its owners, their family's ancestry, and the lives of the countless staff who helped develop and run the house, its gardens and estate. It also highlights periods of cultural isolation when owners stuck with tried and tested methods or domestic historic styles, in contrast to times when the minds of the ruling classes were enlightened by wonders from the Ancient World, or exotic forms from the far corners of the globe.

Each building evolved in a different way. Some have at their heart a medieval timber-framed structure; others, while appearing of the same antiquity, are copies, barely over 100 years old. It will be found that most are not one complete project. The costs of erecting such huge structures in expensive materials, with the finest interior fittings, were so vast that even the wealthiest families often built one part at a time. Many will also show signs of the money having run out; houses with odd proportions or with a wing missing can reflect an over-ambitious owner or cutbacks in the 20th century when aristocratic rule had come to an end.

Despite no one country house being the same as another, there are underlying trends, fashionable layouts and technical developments which can be recognised underneath its unique and personal details. A trip to these wonderful yet bewildering houses can be enlightened if you can recognise familiar forms in the building, date some of the decorative trimmings, and identify from which period the interior fittings belong. This book sets out to empower the reader to do just this, to explain how and why country houses developed and to show the details in the structure which can help date its various parts. My own drawings, diagrams and photographs clearly and concisely convey this information, with a text that focuses on the elements you can see and appreciate today. Any unfamiliar terms are explained or contained in a glossary.

The English Country House Explained is divided into three sections. The first covers five time slots from the late medieval period when country houses first developed up to the 20th century when they began to be boarded up and sold off. Each slot describes the fashionable changes which affected the structure and the interior layout and decoration of the building. The second section goes inside the building and looks at the different styles of interior fittings which can help date them and the changing fashions of the various principal rooms. It also goes behind the green baize door and describes the working hub of the house: the service rooms in which the household staff spent most of their lives and the garden and estate which helped feed, finance and entertain these aristocratic families. Finally, there is a quick reference guide, with details of houses featured in the book and a few others of note which can be visited, the glossary of architectural terms and a list of websites and books for further information.

Trevor Yorke

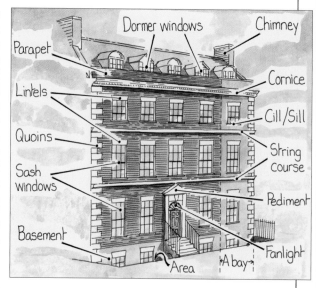

FIG 0.1: *Drawings of an Arts and Crafts (top) and timber-framed house (left) with labels of some of the key elements which can be found on country houses.*

SECTION I

COUNTRY HOUSE STYLES THROUGH THE AGES

Greys Court

CHAPTER I

Chivalry and Gluttony

Late Medieval and Tudor Houses
▦ 1300–1560 ▦

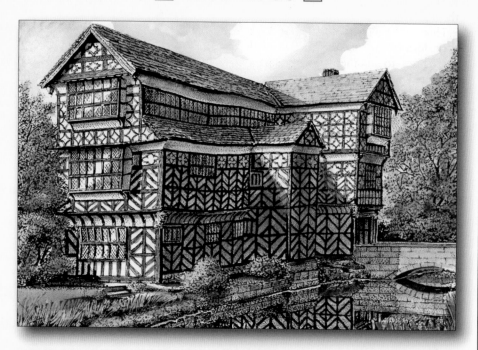

FIG 1.1: LITTLE MORETON HALL, CHESHIRE: *This rambling timber-framed house has, at its core, a 15th-century hall which over the following century was added to, with the famous gatehouse range pictured here being the final piece of the jigsaw in the 1570s. Typically for the period the composition of the house is irregular as rules on symmetry and proportions were unknown to its builder so it did not seem to matter that this main front, with its spectacular row of windows, had a garderobe tower (a toilet block) prominently positioned in the middle!*

To start our journey through the history of the English country house, we need to turn the clock back some 700 years to the Middle Ages. It was a time when military might and the respect it commanded were of primary importance in the life of an aspiring lord of the manor. His household officers were his show of strength, with the size of his personal army and its loyalty to him acting as a barometer of his standing among fellow nobles. He, in return, provided a roof over their heads and regarded them as an extended family.

This community would travel with their lord as he moved from one of his estates to another; a surprisingly frequent event, perhaps occurring every couple of months or so, and involving a huge baggage train in which even the owner's bed was taken along! This portable household, which included a wide social spectrum from young aristocratic knights down to local peasant boys, could number into the hundreds, although many would have been based on one estate and only worked when the lord was visiting. As these medieval manor houses were derived from the castles of the 11th and 12th centuries, they still played the role of a barracks and, hence, most of the household were male, even the entire kitchen staff.

At the head of this family stood the lord, a military leader and faithful Christian, strong in his dispensation of justice, yet hospitable to strangers at his door; a chivalrous and graceful socialite, as much at ease with the dance or the pen as with the horse and sword; and although few would ever have attained this ideal image, these were the expectations heaped on the aspiring noble. Therefore, not only did he have to worry about impressing his guests with huge banquets, feasts and entertainment (anything from half to three-quarters of his total budget would have been spent on food and drink), but he also had to build somewhere to house them and his increasingly large household. By the 15th century, castles and manor houses had been expanded to form the basis of what we would term a country house.

The Style of Houses

In this period the exterior style was not a major consideration in the design of houses. They were laid out with domestic function and military requirements in mind, hence they would appear to be a jumble of buildings set around a courtyard surrounded by crenellated walls, a moat, and accessed through an imposing gatehouse. Even though defensive features would hardly ever be tested in the relatively peaceful counties

FIG 1.2: STOKESAY CASTLE, SHROPSHIRE: *This manor house close to the Welsh border had defensive features like a tower (right) but later additions, as with the 14th-century hall (centre), were more focused on luxury and status.*

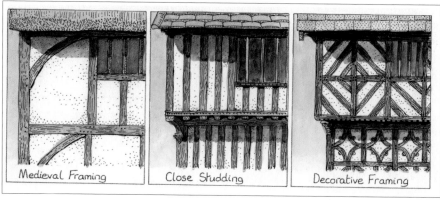

FIG 1.3: *Medieval framing, with its distinctive large panels and thicker, irregular timbers (left), was replaced during the 15th century by close-studding (centre) mainly in the south and east of the country, and small square-framing in the Midlands and the north; the finest with decorative pieces inserted to form elaborate patterns (right and Fig 1.1).*

away from the turbulent border regions, they were used by the owners as statements of power and wealth; some even making their houses in the form of castles and naming them thus.

The buildings were generally vernacular, that is they were built using local materials and craftsmen. Only the wealthiest aristocrats, the Crown and the Church would import stone or use a notable mason or carpenter from outside the region. Most would have constructed the main parts of the house using methods passed down through the generations; with the only concession to fashion appearing in the detailing, like the shape of a window and door, or the style of the timber-framing. Stone from small quarries worked for just the one project tends to be found in highland areas of the north, the west and the limestone belt of central England, with

timber specially reserved for the lord from within his manor being used in most other regions. Although the Romans introduced brick to these shores, after they departed it was not used again until the Late Medieval period, when it became a fashionable material for the finest buildings in the eastern counties.

The Layout of Houses

The plan of the main parts of the house was influenced by the move away from open communal living towards more privacy for the lord and his family, a progressive change which was not complete until the 18th century. The open hall, with a scattering of lesser buildings which was common in the 13th century, had evolved by the 16th into a main house composed of a number of   rooms, with service buildings and lodgings physically attached to it. The increasing size of the household also demanded more rooms, with the senior servants of the lord often receiving their own private lodgings. In many open sites where there were no existing military structures, the main building which was usually an open hall with private rooms at one end (the solar) and service rooms at the other would stand on one side of the main courtyard facing the gatehouse. A chapel and, in some cases, further private chambers, would run along the side nearest the lord's end of the hall, with guest and household accommodation, a brew house (beer was an everyday drink, even consumed at breakfast), stables and a free-standing kitchen (due to the fire risk it posed) making up the rest of the complex.

FIG 1.4. HAMPTON COURT, SURREY:
A medieval country house complex was usually set around a courtyard, with an imposing gatehouse across the entrance, as in this palatial royal building with an oriel window and coat of arms above the doorway.

Exterior Details

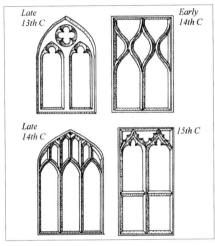

Late 13th C

Early 14th C

Late 14th C

15th C

FIG 1.5: *Most windows were simple and square-headed, with vertical supports called mullions and in taller versions with a horizontal bar called a transom. Important rooms like the end of the hall, however, where the lord of the manor sat (the dais), required something more dramatic and windows with tracery (mirroring the styles on churches) were sometimes fitted. The design of these varied through the period as shown with these examples and can help date the feature. Originally most windows were open to the elements (the word is derived from the Saxon 'wind eye' and their primary purpose was originally ventilation), with only wooden shutters, animal hide or oiled cloth curtains to close them off. Glass was a luxury item which only became common in the finest houses from the 15th century and was of such value that the whole window frame was often taken with the owners as they moved between properties, until the late 16th century when the windows became a fixed part of the house by law.*

FIG 1.7: *Important entrances would have had a stone- or timber-carved arch, in early examples with a distinct point, but as the centuries progressed it became flatter until, by the 16th century, it appears almost straight. The top corners (spandrels) were often filled with decorative carving and heraldic shields, as in this example from Compton Wynyates, Warwickshire, while the moulding along the top continued down the sides (the jambs) finishing short of the bottom in a patterned piece called a stop. Away from the main entrances, door frames were usually part of the structure of the wall and had the door closing onto the back of them and not inset within. The doors themselves were composed of just a few vertical planks often of irregular width held together by horizontal battens across the back (ones with numerous regular timbers are often later replacements). This simple plank and batten door could be enhanced with decorative metal strap hinges, the nails which held it together formed into patterns, or additional pieces of timber added to create a design or to give the door extra strength.*

FIG 1.6: *One place where glass, often decorated with heraldic symbols, could be used to full effect was in an oriel or a bay window. The oriel by the 16th century usually refers to a projecting window from an upper storey although, earlier, the word 'oriole' was applied to porches, staircases and a protrusion into an oratory (from which the word oriel probably evolved). A bay window is one which rests on the ground and runs up more than one storey of the house, although you sometimes find this kind of window still referred to as an oriel. They were most strikingly featured at the dais end of the hall, often replacing a tracery opening as the fashionable window for this position during the 15th century. Not only did they allow more light in than a conventional opening permitted but also allowed those in the hall to peek out and see who was at the door!*

FIG 1.8: BUTTRESSES: *The problem which faced masons was that a sloping roof pushes the walls below it outwards. To counter this, buttresses were placed along the side of the building in line with the roof trusses (the triangular arrangement of beams which support it). These grew deeper through this period and, as builders realised that they were carrying most of the load, the walls could be made thinner and be pierced by larger windows with flatter arches. In the above example the buttresses along the side of the hall (top) line up with the main trusses inside (bottom), although the buttresses are a later addition.*

FIG 1.9: *The dramatic changes to the country house with the creation of private apartments and rooms during the 15th and 16th centuries were only possible in part with the introduction of the chimney (in this period the whole fireplace and stack were called the chimney). Previously, smoke from the fire in the centre of the hall escaped through a louvre opening in the roof which meant there could be no floors above. Despite the use of smoke hoods and bays which set the fire into a corner or end of the room, it was not until the fireplace was positioned against or within a side wall that additional chambers could be fitted above. As smoke from these would be emitted at the lowest part of the roof, a chimney was needed to extend just above the ridge to create a draw. These chimneys became a status symbol, with banks of tall, decorated, polygonal-shaped brick stacks becoming a distinctive feature of Tudor country houses. (Some chimneys were actually false to make it appear the owner had more fireplaces than he did.)*

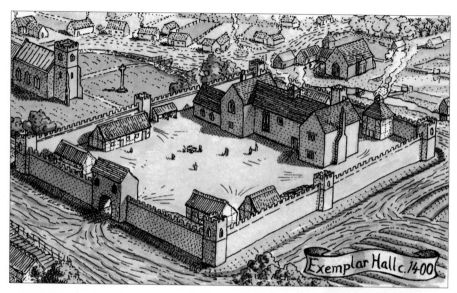

FIG 1.10: EXEMPLAR HALL c.1400: *On our first visit to the imaginary Exemplar Hall the date is 1400 and, after passing by low, timber-framed cottages and a few two-storey houses, you come to the imposing crenellated walls surrounding this manor house. As you turn in and pass under the gatehouse you enter a courtyard surrounded by an array of buildings, with household staff busy crossing between them. The old hall is in front of you, recognisable by its large window and louvre in the roof, while behind it is the kitchen, which is separate from the main building due to its inflammable nature. The impression is of a scattered range of buildings, with the eye drawn to the decorative incidental parts rather than the whole composition. This typical medieval picture had developed slowly through the Middle Ages but in the 16th century things were to change with uncharacteristic speed. The new aristocracy would have different ambitions and motivations, and would use the country house as an expression of these new desires and wealth.*

CHAPTER 2

Wealth and the Humanities

Elizabethan and Jacobean Houses
🔲 1560–1660 🔲

FIG 2.1: HARDWICK HALL, DERBYSHIRE: *This was designed by Robert Smythson, the most famous master mason in the Elizabethan period. Built for Bess of Hardwick from 1591–97, it was radically different from earlier houses with its symmetrical front, roof hidden behind a parapet and a greater area of glass than wall. This outward looking mansion was built to impress, with the owner's initials crowning the dominant towers ('E.S.' stands for Bess's full name, Elizabeth Shrewsbury).*

While our aristocratic families were squabbling over the Crown during the 15th century, far away in Italy a new system of education based upon the study of the Humanities (grammar, rhetoric, history, poetry and moral philosophy) led to a new appreciation of Classical Greek and Roman literature, art, and architecture, a rebirth better known to us as the Renaissance. The effect of this upon 16th-century England was limited, mainly due to the break from Rome and Catholic Europe, which resulted from Henry VIII's quest for a divorce from Catherine of Aragon. Despite this cultural isolation, humanist teachings influenced the upper classes with the new Renaissance gentleman being expected to know Latin and Greek, to have read the scriptures and classics, and to be able to write poetry; while humanist ideals made the acquisition and display of personal wealth more acceptable.

After generations of warfare and plague, the late 16th century marks an upturn in fortunes and no more so than for the gentry. Many aristocrats gained positions of power and influence at Court and increased their wealth by better utilising their estates, perhaps by extracting mineral deposits or enclosing fields, while all benefited from increasing rents and food prices. Many gained new estates after the Dissolution of the Monasteries in the late 1530s although it was not until the relative peace and prosperity under Elizabeth I that the new owners finally knocked down the old monastic buildings and

erected dazzling new houses in their place. The ranks of the upper classes were also being swelled by a new class of lesser gentry, courtiers, merchants, and lawyers, who with a good education and by seizing opportunities had risen to high office.

The coming to the throne in 1603 of James I saw the end of hostilities with Spain and made Europe accessible once again, so that Renaissance ideas could flow more freely from the Continent. During this Jacobean age (from *Jacobus*, the Latin for 'James') there were exponents of Classical architecture but their influence on the country house was not to blossom until after the disruption of the Civil War and the Commonwealth. In this period it is the aristocrat or gentleman, armed with an architectural pattern book from the Continent and a master mason, who were the builders of country houses.

The Style of Houses

The first significant change with the new country houses of the Elizabethan period was that they started to look outwards. Although many were still built around a courtyard, they now had

FIG 2.2: BURGHLEY HOUSE, LINCOLNSHIRE: *Although it appears as a solid mass, this huge prodigy house built for William Cecil over 30 years up to the 1580s is actually a square ring, set around a central courtyard. Numerous windows, prominent displays of chimneys, and ogee-shaped capped towers are typical Elizabethan features.*

a front designed to impress and one which would demonstrate the owner's good taste and wealth. These new houses were also symmetrical, a Renaissance practice derived from the Ancients' belief that as the Gods had made us in the image of themselves so the proportions of the human body were therefore divine, and this included the fact that we, as humans, are symmetrical. Although English builders applied this rule and used numerous classical motifs, they clumsily stacked columns and pediments without having an understanding of the true nature of the rules of proportion and geometry which were being used by designers in Italy.

Another distinction of this period is the obsession with glass. Now that it was more readily available, the country house builder would seemingly use it at every opportunity. The solid mass of medieval walls was replaced by shimmering façades of tall windows. Brick, which was becoming more widespread across the south, east and the Midlands, was still a luxury product and often featured diamond patterns formed of a different colour. Another distinct feature of Elizabethan and Jacobean walls was the use of a continuous entablature or string moulding, a projecting horizontal trim which ran all around the house at the various floor levels.

Prodigy Houses

There was no one dominant style in this period. Many lords built timber-framed structures which were still vernacular but now had a wealth of glass and a few token classical details. However, some of the wealthiest and more cosmopolitan introduced imposing new symmetrical houses in stone and brick. These still resembled castles, having corner towers and gatehouses, but now they had large, vertical, glazed windows, carved classical features and decorative parapets, with strapwork patterns or lettering. These large country houses, usually erected with a visit from the monarch in mind, have been christened Prodigy Houses.

Contacts with our Protestant allies in the Low Countries had already seen the import of details like Dutch gables but in the early 17th century as the restrictions on travel to the Continent were receding, Renaissance ideas flowed more freely. By this stage the architects in Europe had long become bored by the limitations of the strict Classical rules and had started bending

FIG 2.3: WOLLATON HALL, NOTTINGHAM: *This prodigy house, designed by Robert Smythson, has a raised central section with round corner turrets standing above the hall and creates an outline resembling a castle.*

FIG 2.4: *Some owners just updated their earlier house (left) by adding new wings (A), fitting a porch (B) to balance the bay window (C) and inserting a chamber above the hall (D). However, when building from scratch (right) the builder could site the porch centrally (E), with the hall in this case to the left (F), the service rooms to the right or rear (G) and an attic floor (H) for extra accommodation.*

them. This more playful style, labelled as Artisan Mannerism in England, started to bear fruit in the reign of Charles I, only for the Civil War to cut it short. The first great English architect, Inigo Jones, set to work during this Jacobean period but despite his ground-breaking understanding of the principals of Classical architecture, the limited purse strings of the monarchy meant few of his plans ever made it past the drawing board. Inigo Jones's genius would have to wait a hundred years before influencing our country houses.

The Layout of the House

Well-educated Elizabethans loved to communicate in a secret language of symbols and hidden meanings which could even extend to the plan of a house. The E-shaped layout could have implied homage to Queen Elizabeth or to Emmanuel, while the designer John Thorpe even planned a house in the shape of his own initials. Geometric shapes, especially circles, triangles and crosses, could form the basis of the layout. For instance, the triangular lodge at Rushton in Northamptonshire represented the Trinity and symbolised the owner's Catholic faith. In general, an E- or H-shaped plan was common in this period, formed from wings at right angles to the main body which increasingly had a central porch, while the largest houses appear as a massive block but were usually only one main room deep and arranged around a central open area.

The change of role of the country house from the communal centre of a manor to the private residence of a cultured noble can be seen in the layout of both Elizabethan and Jacobean houses. In earlier examples the hall dominated the main part of the house but as it was entered from one end, the

FIG 2.5: LONGLEAT HOUSE, WILTSHIRE: *This was probably the closest that 16th-century England got to a Renaissance house, with its façade a mass of glass, a parapet hiding the roof (A) and a horizontal moulding called a string course (B) and (C) running around the house at each floor level.*

main entrance was sited off centre. As the appreciation of symmetry grew and the hall fell from importance, the room could be re-sited and a central porch positioned in the middle of the façade. At Hardwick (Fig 2.1), for the first time, the hall was turned round end on to the front, making symmetry easier

and thus it became the entrance room with which we associate it today.

With this move to privacy, an ever-increasing ensemble of rooms evolved which could be spread over three rather than two floors. In larger houses there could be a series of state apartments on an upper floor for entertaining and impressing important and, preferably, royal guests. These are usually discernible from the exterior by the row of highest windows. There would then be further private apartments for the family, while the staff still ate in the old hall until as this became an entrance area in the 17th century, a separate servants' hall was provided. The kitchen could now be found within the body of the building since stone and brick fireplaces set within the wall had replaced open hearths for cooking and thus the fire risk was greatly reduced. A fashionable accessory to any aspiring lord's house which is almost exclusive to this period is the long gallery. This was a thin rectangular room which usually spanned the entire length or width of the house, with a bank of windows on one or occasionally both sides.

FIG 2.6: BLICKLING HALL, NORFOLK: *Towers with ogee-shaped caps, Dutch gables (the three in the middle section comprising quadrants and corners) and, on the roof, a white cupola were all popular features in the early 17th century. The tallest windows mark the state apartments which were now often raised above the ground floor as in this example.*

FIG 2.7: *A cut-away view of a modest country house from this period, showing a popular arrangement with the hall on the opposite side of the entrance from the service rooms. The long gallery runs along one of the wings though it could also be found along the length of the house, on the second or third floors.*

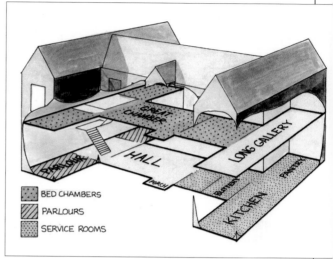

BED CHAMBERS

PARLOURS

SERVICE ROOMS

FIG 2.8: HATFIELD HOUSE, HERTFORDSHIRE: *There is a distinct Renaissance feel to the central section of the south front of this Jacobean house. The arched openings along the ground floor (known as a loggia), the Classical columns and pilasters, and the Dutch gables are all features copied from houses of the period on the Continent. The pairs of columns up the sides of the central porch are typical of the late 16th and early 17th centuries.*

Exterior Details

FIG 2.10: *The chimneys in this period tended to have individual stacks for each fireplace below them joined at the top, and were often found in rows like this example. Brick and stone were used for their construction, often with prominent bands linking them at the top. By the 17th century they began to become less prominent.*

FIG 2.9: *A typical 16th/early 17th-century window from a country house. The windows were almost exclusively square or rectangular frames, with a number of fixed horizontal (transoms) and vertical bars (mullions). As there was not the technology yet to make large pieces of glass, the windows were filled with small panes held in place by lead strips in a diamond pattern with metal stanchions up the centre on the inside to prevent damage.*

FIG 2.11: *This corner tower is a common feature of 16th- and early 17th-century houses. Of brick construction, with stone corner blocks (quoins) and a cap in a distinctive 'S' profile (ogee).*

FIG 2.13: *Brickwork with a 'diaper' pattern made from darker bricks which were vitrified by over burning or the addition of salt in the firing stage of their construction. Bricks of this period were often hand-made on site and were usually thinner and longer than modern machine-made examples. The pattern formed on the face of the wall by the differing arrangements of bricks is known as bonding and, in this period, English bond which was formed from alternate layers of headers (the short end of the brick) and stretchers (the long side) was popular.*

FIG 2.12: *The humble entrance to the medieval house was superseded in this period by flamboyant, if sometimes clumsy, porches. They are discernible by their height and narrowness, and by the stacked series of Classical ornaments and columns with a round headed doorway below. This example on the north front of Lyme Park, Cheshire, incorporates all these features although the top section with the statue was added at a later date.*

FIG 2.14: *The parapet along the top of walls hid the roof from view and gave the building a more imposing, Classical form. In this period many were punctuated with initials (as in the top of the towers at Hardwick in Fig 2.1) or, as in this case, with actual words made out of stone.*

FIG 2.15: *This pattern of swirls and straights formed by flat pieces of masonry slightly raised above the surrounding stone wall is known as strapwork. It was popular between 1580 and 1620, and can be found decorating both exterior and interior features.*

FIG 2.16: EXEMPLAR HALL c.1600: *Two hundred years have passed since we last visited Exemplar Hall and the recent lords of the manor have made modest progress and have embellished their family home rather than rebuilding it. The entrance is marked by an impressive brick gatehouse, with the courtyard beyond now lined with new lodgings and service buildings. A small concession to symmetry appears on the front of the main hall which has a large bay window to the left and a tall porch balancing it to the right. A new kitchen has been built on the right side of the house and the area at the rear, where it previously stood, has now become a garden.*

Modest country houses like this for the gentry were still amateur attempts at architecture, a sometimes clumsy mix of traditional English forms, with the latest in foreign Classical decoration. From the 1660s a new breed of aristocrat and artisan, better acquainted with the theory and styles of European architecture, was to design new forms of houses with bold, deep structures and carefully planned layouts which would now be emulated by the lesser gentry.

CHAPTER 3

Commerce and Science

❖

Restoration and William and Mary Houses
▦ 1660–1720 ▦

FIG 3.1: BELTON HOUSE, LINCOLNSHIRE: *This late 17th-century house is similar to Clarendon House in London, by Roger Pratt which, along with Coleshill in Berkshire, influenced the design of numerous country houses in this period. Belton was built rapidly between 1684 and 1687. Surprisingly, its mentor Clarendon House only lasted seventeen years, being demolished the year before Belton was started.*

Religious and constitutional differences erupted into civil war in 1642 and, after the subsequent Parliamentary victory, a large number of aristocrats and gentry lay dead or had fled abroad to France and the Low Countries, only returning from exile when the Monarchy was restored in 1660. The population welcomed Charles II but Parliament was more cautious and limited his powers and purse strings, hence he relied on the French King Louis XIV for financial support.

In a period of religious tensions with the Puritans at one end of the spectrum and the Papists (Roman Catholics) at the other, Charles trod a careful diplomatic line, only revealing his true faith on his deathbed. Although he had kept his Catholic leanings secret, his brother James II who succeeded him in 1685 did not, and the birth of James's son was one of the triggers which inspired a group of lords to invite the Protestant William of Orange, the husband of Charles II's daughter Mary, to invade and claim the throne. The subsequent constitutional changes known as the Glorious Revolution increased parliamentary powers and gave the aristocracy supremacy over the monarch. As a result, they gained the opportunity to further their wealth, especially with perks from their new positions of office. With its new powers, Parliament had regular sittings rather than just being recalled by the monarch when money was needed. Thus, a social season developed when the gentry and their entourage invaded London, many leaving their country houses during the winter to rent new fashionable urban properties. Some aristocrats, however, went in the other direction, making additional income by putting tenants in their London homes and concentrating efforts on developing their country estates now there was sufficient political stability to give them confidence to build on a large scale.

This was also the period of commercial revolution and many of the upper classes grew rich on foreign enterprise. Science also blossomed, heightened by a desire to understand and control Nature in the face of what many believed was the impending 'end of the world'. The gulf between the cultured gentleman, with his new scientific learning, and his illiterate household staff, still influenced by medieval superstitions, widened further. The building of the house within which they all resided was still likely to be the project of the owner, but now he was aided by an architect, not necessarily a full-time professional but an educated gentleman who may have

FIG 3.2: SUDBURY HALL, DERBYSHIRE: *A house primarily of the 1660s and '70s which looks backwards as much as forward. Despite the fashionable features on this south front like the cupola, parapet, dormer windows and plain rectangular chimneys, it has by this time outdated details like diaper-patterned brickwork and Jacobean-style mullioned windows. This may be due to the tastes of the owner, George Vernon, who, like some at the time, still acted as his own architect.*

studied the fashionable building styles on the Continent and grasped the principles of Classical architecture. They were rarely educated in this art. John Vanbrugh, for instance, had been a captain in the Marines, while Christopher Wren practised anatomy, yet these men of ingenuity replaced masons and carpenters as the designers of country houses.

The Style of House

The returning monarch and his court in 1660 brought with them from France and the Low Countries, a taste for the latest in Classical architecture, new designs which dominated this period such that few gentlemen would consider building their manor houses in a vernacular style. The most distinctive type of country house in this period evolved from the work of Inigo Jones, what little there was, from Coleshill in Berkshire, built in the early 1650s by Sir Roger Pratt (but now demolished), and from the Dutch Palladian-style of houses which was seen by those exiled in Holland. These had a plain façade with quoins (raised corner stones), two rows of tall but roughly equal-sized windows and a deep overhanging white cornice. Above this was a prominent hipped roof, broken up by lines of dormer windows, stout rectangular chimneys, and often crowned by a cupola (see Fig 3.3).

Baroque

Many architectural styles have their name coined by the next generation of designers as an insult to what they regard as an outdated or inappropriate

FIG 3.3: UPPARK, SUSSEX. *The façade of this Dutch-style house is capped by a hipped roof (A), with plain rectangular chimneys (B), and dormer windows (C), a pediment (D) and a deep cornice (E). The lower of the two rows of tall windows (F) are slightly higher, indicating that this floor contains the principal rooms while the half-height windows below (G) illuminate the basement.*

fashion. In this case, later critics labelled the largest buildings of the late 17th and early 18th centuries with their fanciful shapes, opulent decoration and irregular skyline, Baroque, after the French word barocco, meaning 'a mis-shaped pearl'. This style had its origins in the 16th-century reforms of the Catholic Church in reaction to the threat from Protestantism in which a new form of art evolved which was designed to stupefy and impress upon the viewer the everlasting and unchanging nature of Heaven. A good example of this change can be seen in portraits: from the rather flat Elizabethan gentleman standing

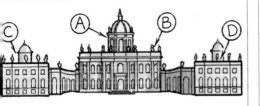

FIG 3.4: CASTLE HOWARD, YORKSHIRE: *The dome (A) and statues along the parapet (B), along with the variation in height, make a dramatic skyline to this famous Baroque house. The main body of the building in the centre is flanked by two separate wings (C) for the service rooms and (D) originally designed as stables but built for accommodation thirty years later.*

FIG 3.5: BLENHEIM PALACE, OXFORDSHIRE: *The central body of this monumental Baroque house was designed primarily by John Vanbrugh. Note the tall windows, now with glazing bars rather than transoms and mullions, the arched heads to those on the top row and the round windows along the basement. Giant pilasters (columns attached to the wall) and the busy decoration of the portico (the pediment supported on columns across the entrance) are typical of this period.*

upright with his hand on hip, to Van Dyke's portrait of Charles I on his bucking horse produced only a few decades later, a new dynamic visualisation full of movement with sweeping vistas and flying angels. This change would also be mirrored in architecture as many aristocrats turned to France for inspiration in creating a dramatic, grand and imposing style of country house.

The houses built in this style from the late 1600s like Blenheim and Castle Howard were monumental in scale, with façades which step or curve in and out, and a skyline of pinnacles and towers which owes as much to the medieval castle as to Continental sources. Other houses of this brief English Baroque period may have been, like Chatsworth, a piecemeal reconstruction, or just a re-faced existing building which in either case limited the shape of the structure. It is in the detailing of the façade where the style shines through. Entrances flanked by oversized blocks, tall windows some with rounded tops, heavy surrounds to openings in the wall, and a stone balustrade along the roof featuring Classical urns or statues (hiding the now lower chimneys) are some of the popular features.

The Layout of the House

The major change in the layout of country houses after the Restoration was the adoption of a double pile plan,

FIG 3.6: CHATSWORTH HOUSE, DERBYSHIRE: *William Talman designed this new Baroque-styled south front (top) for the Duke of Devonshire in 1687, with its distinctive giant pilasters and vases along the parapet. By the time the owner came to rebuild the west front (bottom,) he had fallen out with Talman and this was probably the work of the Duke, aided by his masons, with the central pediment containing the coat of arms, a common feature at this time (completed in 1702).*

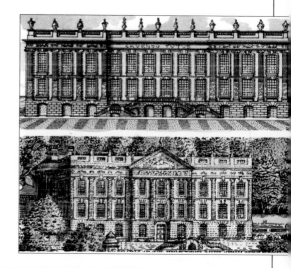

that is, one which is two rooms deep. By the end of this period it had also became universal to have a basement. The advantage of this being that as the social gulf between the gentry and their staff had now widened, it was convenient to place the engine room of the house out of sight, along with its smells and noise. The basement also had a stone or brick vaulted ceiling to reduce the fire risk from the kitchen. As there would have to be some light in these service rooms, a row of low windows was inserted which meant that the rooms could not be built completely below ground. In turn, this meant that the ground floor of the house was raised, thus having the desirable effect of making the entrance, now up a row of exterior steps, more impressive to the visitor. At the top of the house, attic floors were standard in the Dutch-style houses. With their massive sloping roofs, a row of small, wedged-shaped

windows called dormers sticking out of the tiles was the only way of lighting these rooms. With accommodation now spread over four floors, the actual ground plan of the house could become more compact. The arrangement of the rooms also changes during the 17th century. Houses like Coleshill still had the state apartments on the first floor and they would be approached up an ever more elaborate staircase, sometimes rising out of the hall itself, relegating it to its present role of a reception room. Access to the rooms from the staircases could now be via corridors rather than through rooms as in previous periods. A spinal one which ran the full length of the house sandwiched between the front and back rows of rooms was common, reflecting the symmetry of the exterior.

In the later Baroque houses it became usual to have the state apartments on the ground floor so the grand staircase

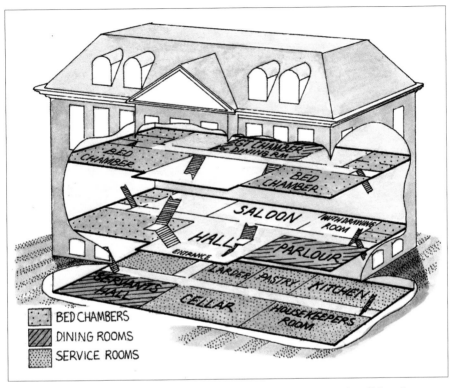

FIG 3.7: *A cut-away view of an imaginary Restoration house which still has the state apartments on the first floor, the family rooms on the ground and the service rooms in the basement.*

in the hall was no longer required. Instead, the guests walked directly through to the saloon behind and, from here, could turn left or right to access the luxurious withdrawing rooms and bed chambers. It became fashionable to have these rooms laid out one after the other along the rear of the house, with the doorways all in line, an arrangement known as the enfilade, the length of which in this period of processions and ceremonies became something of a status symbol. The larger Baroque houses further emphasised their monumental scale by having separate courtyards to the side of the central house or flanking the entrance area. One would usually contain the service rooms like the kitchen, separated from the dining room to reduce the fire risk and the odours and noise, with the other courtyard usually housing the stables and coach houses.

FIG 3.8: *An example of an enfilade. Note that in this Baroque house the principal rooms are on the ground floor so that a huge staircase in the hall is no longer required. Discreetly positioned stairs lead up to the family's private rooms.*

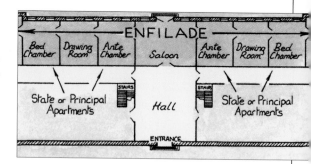

Exterior Details

FIG 3.9: *Square-headed doors and windows could be capped with a segmental arch (left) or a triangular pediment resting upon scrolled brackets, with these options often alternated along a façade or on the dormer windows in the roof. Baroque houses would have more imposing doorways with, in this case, the pediment broken by a huge keystone. The horizontal grooves cut into the side pillars are a style of decoration known as rustication; a favourite decoration of the architect John Vanbrugh.*

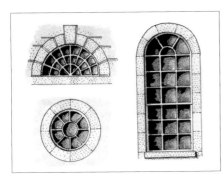

FIG 3.10: *A selection of arched and round windows from Baroque houses.*

FIG 3.12: *A common feature on Dutch-styled houses was a deep overhanging cornice with carved brackets and moulding. Above this, a row of dormer windows, with alternate triangular and arched pediments, was popular.*

FIG 3.11: *From the 1680s, sash windows appear for the first time and quickly become popular. It is hazardous to try and date a country house from the style of window as they were frequently changed at a later date but, in general, the older sash windows have thicker glazing bars and frames, with more numerous lights (the individual opening between the glazing bars).*

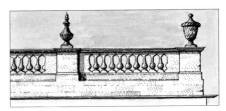

FIG 3.13: *A section of parapet which crowned the top of this Baroque house helped to hide the roof and chimneys. The vases standing on top, which could have equally been statues, gave the house a distinctive skyline.*

FIG 3.14: *Classical scrolls and swags of flowers and fruit were a popular form of decoration inside and out during the late 17th and early 18th centuries.*

FIG 3.15: *A stone cupola mounted as a central feature on the roof and granting the owner and his guests views over his surrounding parkland. These were usually domed, often with balustrades around the edge of the flat roof on which they stood and were very popular in the second half of the 17th century. Unfortunately, many were later removed along with the balustrades when a house was restyled.*

FIG 3.16: EXEMPLAR HALL c.1700: *Over the past century the rambling collection of medieval buildings has been swept aside to make way for a new symmetrical Dutch-style house, with only the old chapel and the wall between it and the church retained. To the right the site has expanded out into what were previously fields and a new stable courtyard with an arched entrance has been erected. Behind the house the garden has been terraced and the main estate farm has been masked off by trees and landscaping as the lord of the manor began separating himself from the village both socially and physically. Yet within a generation, this flamboyant style of building would seem outdated and inappropriate and in turn would be replaced by new, strict forms of Classicism and a scale of country house which would result in great upheavals to the communities and landscape around them.*

CHAPTER 4

Liberty and Sensibility

❖

Georgian Houses

🔳 1720–1800 🔳

FIG 4.1: LYME PARK, CHESHIRE: *The south front of this Tudor mansion was designed in the 1720s by Giacomo Leoni in the new Palladian style, with rusticated masonry along the lower section, tall windows on the first floor illuminating the piano nobile, and a portico in the centre capped off by a plain triangular pediment. The pilasters, though, could have been found on Baroque houses.*

Those who had supported the exclusion of James II from the Crown and had welcomed the subsequent Glorious Revolution in 1688 had risen in power. In 1715, after the accession to the throne of George I,

they removed great swathes of the old landed gentry from high office. These Whigs (from the word *Whiggamore*, a term for Scottish Covenanters who had also opposed James II) were to dominate the developing political map during the 18th century, excluding the Tories (from the word *toriadhe*, which was Irish for an outlaw, an insult aimed at supporters of James II) from office until the accession of George III. It was these aristocrats in high office rather than the reclusive Hanoverian monarchs who were the cultural leaders of their day.

The Whigs under Robert Walpole, the first so-called Prime Minister, claimed to be champions of commerce and investment, fighting for liberty as opposed to tyrannical rule. They imagined themselves as senators in Imperial Rome, complete with toga and olive crown, rather than just country gentlemen. They sent their sons off on grand tours of Italy where they not only soaked up the wonders of Ancient Rome but also brought cart loads of it back with them, often one of the reasons for the family country house being extended. The 18th-century aristocrat thus developed from a collector of curiosities into an art connoisseur, amassing books and prints rather than displays of arms. He joined societies devoted perhaps to ancient architecture or archaeology, and opened his mind to emotions and an appreciation of the beauty and drama to be found in nature. In other words it became acceptable to be a bit of a sensitive chap.

This lifestyle did not come cheap, and these gentlemen would benefit from some understanding of developments in science, industry and agriculture to increase their incomes, especially from their country estates which, for many, were their main financial source.

Improvement was the order of the day and enclosure of the fields on their land was one of the most controversial and still visible marks that it made. The new houses they built and the older ones which were extended were only possible because of their growing wealth and status. The old Tory squires and repressed Catholic families, however, deprived of the incomes which came with holding office, often had to make do with their old compact Tudor and Jacobean piles.

In the second half of the 18th century, with the defeat of France in 1763 and London now the chief financial centre, there were many commercial gains to be made. Aristocratic sons set off for adventure on the high seas, took up posts abroad, developed quarries, mines and factories and established trading companies, returning with great wealth to enhance their family's estates. This period of rapid development was halted by the French Revolution of 1793 and the subsequent war with Napoleon as, for the first time, aristocratic families and the ruling classes felt insecure. Suddenly, liberty and sensibility with their French associations seemed inappropriate.

The Style of Houses

This era is dominated by Classical architecture which by the end of the period was being manipulated by professional rather than amateur architects. Few houses were built in any other style until the last decades of the century, and the Ancients' rules of proportion and architectural orders

FIG 4.2: CHISWICK HOUSE, LONDON: *This startling villa was designed by the Earl of Burlington from 1723–29. He promoted the architecture of Palladio and its later interpretation by Inigo Jones and statues of the two men stand at the base of the stairs (just out of view). The plan of the house is square with a symmetrical layout of rooms, aesthetically pleasing but not so practical for everyday use.*

even filtered down to terraced houses. To the refined Georgian aristocrat, good taste was of primary importance, and his country house would reflect this in its reserved and strict adherence to these Classical rules and orders. Only later in the period would it become acceptable again to bend the rules as Baroque architects had previously done.

Palladian

In the opening years of the reign of George I, a dramatically new style of house started to appear across the country, one which was principally used by, and has since been associated with, the new Whig aristocrats. This style was championed by two men: Colen Campbell and Lord Burlington, who were determined to remove the flamboyant excesses of the Baroque and return to pure Classical architecture as determined by the Roman Vitruvius and the later Renaissance architects. They helped rediscover the drawings and work of Inigo Jones and championed the plans of the late 16th-century Italian architect Andraes Palladio, after whom this new Palladian style was named.

The first influential building in this new style was Wanstead House, London, (demolished 1824) by Colen Campbell. It introduced the characteristic Palladian façade, with a rusticated masonry base (stonework with deep grooves or rough surface) below the first floor or piano nobile, which housed the state apartments and was identified by a long line of tall rectangular windows with smaller ones above. A shallow pitched roof either overhanging with a decorative cornice or hidden behind a plain parapet finished the top of the wall, while chimneys, now that most houses had them, became nothing to show off so were low and kept out of view. Most significant was the portico, a huge triangular pediment supported on columns, which acted as an enormous storm porch marking the main entrance to the house which was reached up a grand staircase from below. Gone were the flowing, undulating lines of the Baroque mansions; now, plain, refined horizontal blocks with temple-like centre pieces were the order of the day for the gentleman of taste. Their beauty lay in the strict adherence to the rules of proportion, with decoration limited to carvings along the cornice and the top of the columns. Palladio had also developed other designs which proved popular – a square plan with porticos on one or all four sides and a central dome above as used at Chiswick House – while a main rectangular block with individual wings linked by a colonnade or corridor inspired buildings like Kedleston Hall in Derbyshire.

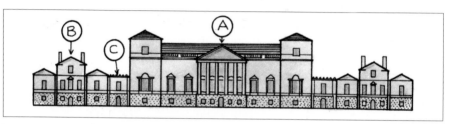

FIG 4.3: HOLKHAM HALL, NORFOLK: *Rather than the Baroque practice of massing blocks and curves up to a crescendo in the middle, the large Palladian house is composed of separate, symmetrical sections. The main house (A) with a large portico in the middle and a tower at each end is similar to Wilton House in Wiltshire, designed by Inigo Jones nearly 100 years before. The wings (B) at each end are linked to the main house, in this case, by enclosed corridors (C).*

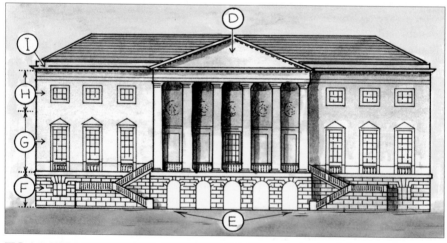

FIG 4.4: KEDLESTON HALL, DERBYSHIRE: *The main body of the north front, with its distinctive Palladian features of a prominent portico (D) upon a base broken by arches and with stairs (E) either side, a rusticated masonry base (F) and tall first floor windows (G) marking the piano nobile. Further rooms above are distinguished by a row of square windows (H) while the top is finished off with a cornice (I), one of the few areas of decoration on these otherwise plain fronts.*

Neo Classical Houses

The new generation of architects who appeared in the mid 18th century found strict adherence to Palladio's pattern book too limiting. They wanted to be more imaginative and creative so they began to look at other periods of history for inspiration, helped along by new archaeological discoveries. Until now, houses were based on Renaissance interpretations or simply on guesses as to what a Roman house would have looked like. For instance, Palladio thought that they all had a portico on the front, so Campbell and his followers in their quest for historic accuracy stuck them on every building. It was only as the societies, which these architects and their patrons helped establish, funded excavations in places like Pompeii that it became clear that, in fact, Roman houses did not have porticos on the front. The new architects increasingly by-passed

FIG 4.5: KEDLESTON HALL, DERBYSHIRE: *The south front was completed some years after the north by Robert Adam in a Neo Classical style. Although the sides mirror the earlier work, the centrepiece is based on an actual Roman triumphal arch rather than upon Palladio's designs. It features Adam's distinctive shallow and delicate decorative details.*

Palladio's works and went straight to these new archaeological sources for their inspiration. At the same time Nicholas Revett and James Stuart produced the first accurate drawings of Ancient Greek buildings in Athens and although the limited range of Greek forms did not immediately appeal to architects craving greater variety, they did add Greek orders and detailing to their increasing architectural palette. The country houses which used these newly-discovered Roman and Greek forms from the 1760s onwards are labelled Neo (New) Classical.

Another difference between Neo Classical houses and the previous Palladian buildings is a return to the more playful use of Ancient architecture. Robert Adams, the most prolific country house architect of this period, believed that the Romans themselves had bent the rules. He set about adding a sense of movement and space to his façades although he despised the Baroque use of flamboyant decoration to hide the function of the building. Features to look out for are curved bay windows, flat domes, columns standing proud of the front and shallow arched recesses. Stone was the must-have material for these new houses (often only a thin cladding) and when it wasn't available, brick, which had still been acceptable in Palladian houses, was covered in stucco, a smooth rendered finish, grooved and coloured to appear like stone.

The Layout of Houses

Throughout the 18th century there was an increased demand for space as

FIG 4.6: SHUGBOROUGH HALL, STAFFORDSHIRE: *A Neo Classical façade but with evidence of two previous styles showing through. The three-storey main block was built in the 1690s, onto which wings were added either side in a Palladian style some 50 years later. Samuel Wyatt redesigned it in the 1790s, adding the large, flat-topped portico and a balustrade running at the same level along the façade. This emphasised the horizontal lines which were a key component of a Classical house and held together the various elements from which the front was composed.*

FIG 4.7: TATTON PARK, CHESHIRE: *This mansion was rebuilt in stages by Samuel and Lewis Wyatt from 1780–1813 in the Neo Classical style. The recessed shallow arches above the outer windows, the swag motifs in the centre and the lack of decoration around the windows are typical features of a house of this date.*

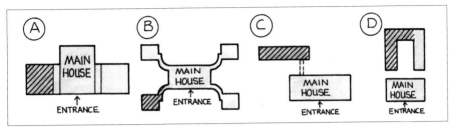

FIG 4.8: *Four plans of 18th-century country houses, with the shaded areas showing the possible position of the service rooms: (A) has two wings in line with the front of the house, while (B) has the popular layout for the larger house with four linked pavilions; (C) has the service rooms in a separate building which could be linked by a passage or even a tunnel; while in (D) a courtyard to the north of the house allows the sun to shine on the other three faces of the more compact country house while the working area is cool.*

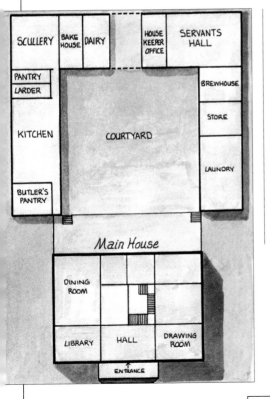

aristocrats opened their doors to a wider range of guests, rather than just exclusive dignitaries, and hosted numerous parties. They also had to house all the art works they were bringing back from the Continent and install a library to store their collection of books, as well as setting aside more specialist areas for the production and preparation of food. This wider range of rooms, however, was restricted in size and layout by the Classical orders and symmetry of the façades, while the interior spaces were also controlled by the desire to make them in the correct proportions.

FIG 4.9: *A plan of a compact country house from the late Georgian period, with a separate courtyard containing the service rooms. This area often incorporates older parts of the building or masks an earlier front of the main house.*

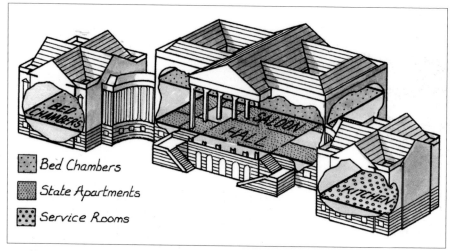

Bed Chambers

State Apartments

Service Rooms

FIG 4.10: *A cut-away view of a Palladian house. The hall, with a saloon behind it, forms the axis of the house with, as near as possible, a symmetrical arrangement of rooms off either side. Above these state apartments could be found bed chambers although some further family or guest rooms might be located in one of the pavilions off to the side. The kitchen is in one of these to reduce the fire and odour risk, although some store rooms like the cellar or butler's pantry would remain in the basement of the main house.*

For the larger house a main block with the principal rooms on a raised ground floor could have separate pavilions at each side, connected by corridors or just an open colonnaded passage (a row of columns), with additional accommodation in one and service rooms in the other. Although this impressive design had the advantage of keeping the odours and noises from the kitchen at bay, it was likely that diners in the main house would be receiving their meals cold. Most medium and smaller country houses were still built as a rectangular block, some retaining the 17th-century habit of siting the service rooms in the basement; while others created separate ranges of buildings for them set back to one side or forming a courtyard at the rear of the house. These tended to be closer to the dining room so there would be some heat in the meals by the time they arrived at the table. However, this unwelcome carbuncle growing out of one side would have to be disguised by careful landscaping and planting! The square plan used at Chiswick House, London and Mereworth Castle, Kent was inflexible in its layout and created difficulty in accommodating service rooms especially if the house was to be viewed on all four sides. Thus, this limited its popularity.

Exterior Details

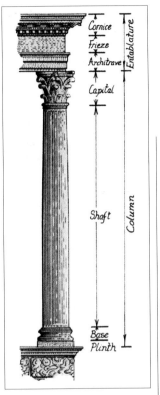

FIG 4.11: *A Classical column (in the Corinthian order) listing the parts from which it is composed. Although the various orders had differing proportions and detailing, it is the style of the capital which easily distinguishes one from another. The shaft could be plain or fluted (vertical grooves are shown in this example,) whilst the Tuscan order was always plain.*

FIG 4.12: *The Corinthian order (top left) was first used by the Greeks but was more popular with the Romans and hence it appears in England from the 16th century. The Ionic order with scrolls was used by the Romans (bottom right) and the Greeks (middle left) and again appears here from the 16th century, while the Composite order incorporates both Corinthian and Ionic. The Roman Doric order (top right) had plain rings and was similar to the Tuscan order, while the Greek version (middle right) had a shallow angled ring directly on a fluted column and as these were recorded from the mid 18th century they became distinctive of Neo Classical houses.*

FIG 4.13: *Sash windows were almost universal in the 18th century. During this period they have increasingly thinner glazing bars, larger panes of glass, and have their outer frame recessed within and, by the late 18th century, hidden behind the wall.*

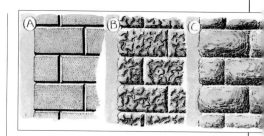

FIG 4.15: *Rusticated masonry could either be smooth, with chamfered 'V'-shaped grooves (A), vermiculated with curved channels (B), or cyclopean which is left with a rough hewn finish (C) as if it had been cut out of the very rock the house was built on.*

FIG 4.14: *A classic compact Palladian-style house (on the Chatsworth estate), with the distinctive gable end wings and a row of square sashes above the main floors. The tall arched windows flanked by lower rectangular ones in the wings are Venetian and were very popular on Palladian and Neo Classical houses.*

FIG 4.16: *Robert Adam is notable as the first architect to really design the whole house from the exterior down to interior details. It formed a distinct style which still carries his name today. His exteriors are distinguished by swags, oval features, round medallions, and Greek decoration, with most mouldings shallow and delicate.*

FIG 4.17: *Many country houses from the mid 18th century were a bit of a sham with stone cladding as in this example, where it was used to cover up older brickwork or stucco (a type of render) being used to make houses appear more up-to-date.*

FIG 4.18: *This pavilion from Stowe House, Buckinghamshire, was designed by Robert Adam in 1771. It features shallow blank arches which can cover a number of windows or even a complete front, and decorative garlands and round medallions which were characteristic of houses in the late 18th century and early 19th century.*

FIG 4.19: *A panel with a garland; in this case, of oak leaves, held by ribbons tied in a bow and a swag which was a common Neo Classical motif.*

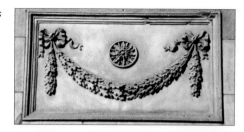

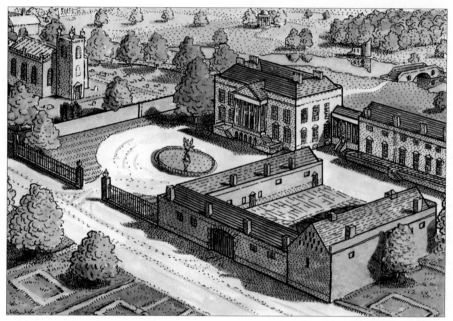

FIG 4.20: EXEMPLAR HALL c.1800: *The owners of Exemplar Hall have made few changes to the main house other than to give it a Classical makeover, fitting a portico on the front and building a new wing to the right to provide extra accommodation. They have dramatically changed its surroundings, however, with the old village cleared out of the way to form a new landscaped garden and the river flooded to make a picturesque lake. Only the old parish church survives and, as it holds the family memorials, it has been rebuilt in a Classical style.*

This period of intense building and gardening was to slow down in the last decades of the 18th century due to war, firstly with America and then France. When stability returned there were new gentlemen, who had grown rich on commercial and industrial profit, entering the ranks of the aristocracy, while the search for a suitable national style and influences from an expanding empire combined to change the face of the country house in its last and most glorious period of development.

CHAPTER 5

Empire and Industry

❖

Regency, Victorian and Edwardian Houses
▨ 1800–1914 ▨

FIG 5.1: CAPESTHORNE HALL, CHESHIRE: *At first glance the brick exterior with ogee-shaped caps upon square towers, Dutch gables, and mullioned windows looks like a Jacobean mansion. It is, in fact, a house of 1719 which was rebuilt in 1837 by Edward Blore in a pseudo Jacobean style. Often it is only on close inspection of details like brickwork and windows that these Victorian imitations can be told apart from the originals.*

The French Revolution and the subsequent war with France heralded in a period of change. In reaction to the threat from Napoleon, England became severed from Europe and became fiercely patriotic, with a number of country houses built like castles. Enlightened thoughts and sensibilities were quickly replaced by hard commercial facts and industrial ingenuity, to which even the old landed families had succumbed by the 1830s. In addition to the income from agricultural rents which had supported the needs of their predecessors could now be added profits from mines, mills, factories (these often built on their country estates), railways, canals, docks and shipping, investments in stocks and shares, and rent from urban developments. Despite the wealth they amassed, it became increasingly easy to lose it all as huge sums were spent on a daughter's dowry, running election campaigns, maintaining a hunt, gambling (especially horse racing), entertaining shooting parties and on increasingly grand houses to accommodate this busy social life. Although most of the landed gentry protected their family estates and avoided splitting them between siblings, those who did get into financial difficulty could find gentlemen who aspired to join the aristocracy and so were eager to snap up the property or were willing to marry into the family so that they could rise to the top rank in society.

By the middle of the 19th century the image of the aristocrat was changing. Revolution throughout Europe in the first half of the century had awoken them to the need to take more of the populace under their wing in order to hang onto power and hence their fortunes. They were the cultural leaders of their day and passed their moral codes down to an aspiring middle-class especially through public schools. The ideal gentleman would be a devout Christian and a good landlord, could be a supporter of the arts and of improvements in health and education,

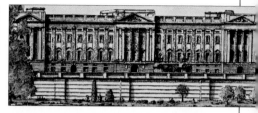

FIG 5.2: BUCKINGHAM PALACE, LONDON: *One of the great monuments of the patriotic Regency period dating from 1825–1830. It was, in fact, a rebuilding of the existing Buckingham House by John Nash for George IV, whose notoriety for extravagance was well founded and the architect's reputation was tarnished by the expenditure lavished on this project.*

but above all would be a faithful husband and family man.

In reality, many had lost interest in industry and commerce with which their fathers had made their fortunes and instead entered political service. They were more likely to be seen enjoying themselves, hunting, shooting, smoking and playing billiards. No longer did they collect Classical artefacts. Instead, the 19th-century gentleman would fill his rooms with antique furniture, family paintings, Persian rugs and house plants, while exotic trees from around the world adorned his garden. He could also succumb to the new national obsession with history, as less was being written about innovation and more about the past, especially the perceived highly religious and moral Middle Ages. The search for a national identity had fused in an isolationist, mystical world of valiant knights and worthy craftsmen

FIG 5.3: HIGHCLERE CASTLE, HAMPSHIRE: *This backdrop for TV's* Downton Abbey *was designed by Charles Barry shortly after he had completed plans for the new Houses of Parliament in the late 1830s. Unlike that Gothic-inspired piece, Highclere echoes the Renaissance style of the late 16th century (see Fig 2.3) with its castle form decorated with Italianate details and strapwork.*

which was probably as much a reaction against machines and a fear of the new than a quest for the origins of English democracy. The Victorians had found merry old England on their doorstep and an empire that was the envy of all other nations. Now at home they transferred the architecture from a favourite period or fashionable country onto their country houses.

The Style of Houses

Until now, country houses have fitted into fairly neat periodic groupings, with the odd whim of an owner an exception and not a rule. However, from the turn of the 19th century, architects found it acceptable to pluck details from a wider variety of sources which in some cases was just a few exotic or historic details that quickly developed into the complete structure. There was also a growing appreciation of the picturesque, inspired by Classical landscape painting, with lakes bordered by rugged mountains, waterfalls and ruined buildings which had been the blueprint for 18th-century landscape

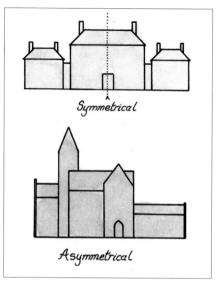

FIG 5.4: *A symmetrical 18th-century Palladian house (top) and an asymmetrical Victorian Gothic one (bottom).*

lighter slates for roofing which meant that flatter pitched roofs could be fitted; and oil, gas and later electricity providing lighting. As architecture started to blend with engineering, so iron posts and girders could be found lurking behind the brick or stone façade.

The period from 1800–1837 which is loosely termed Regency (although the Prince Regent only ruled as such in his father's absence between 1811–1820) is notable for a wide selection of styles inspired by the drama of native ruins, new discoveries from Ancient Egypt and increased contact with the Far East. It was acceptable to deceive and imitate, most notably with brick walls covered in stucco and then scoured and painted to match fashionable stonework. The details of the house also become more delicate, with

gardens and follies. Now, some country houses were being designed as if they had been plucked from one of these pictures, freeing the architect from the strict rules of symmetry and proportion so that picturesque houses could use a variety of textures and shapes and, most notably, could be asymmetric. It was also the association made with the choice of style and site. For instance, a castle built on top of a rocky outcrop implies power, strength, solidity and inspires awe, which was more important than the architectural detail viewed closer at hand. Another factor which affected houses was the new materials and technology available: large panes of glass for windows;

FIG 5.5: NETHER WINCHENDON HOUSE, BUCKINGHAMSHIRE:
This ancient house received a Regency make over in the latest Gothick fashion which included facing much of the timber-framed parts in stone. Note the period features like the stout pointed windows with Y-shaped glazing bar, battlements and a balcony between the two nearest towers.

thinner glazing bars in the windows and intricate patterns formed by cast-iron used in balconies and verandas.

Gothick (the 'k' at the end differentiating it from the later Victorian Gothic) was a rather whimsical interpretation of medieval buildings. It was first applied to a complete house at Strawberry Hill, Twickenham, the home of Horace Walpole (youngest son of the first Prime Minister Robert Walpole). His restyling of this house from 1750 was a breakthrough in its asymmetrical design and use of Gothic details, which reflected the growing interest in romantic ruins of abbeys and castles. From 1790 a few architects produced new Gothick country houses with this more irregular layout, though for many this was purely applied to existing properties or new extensions. Details to look for are steeply-pitched

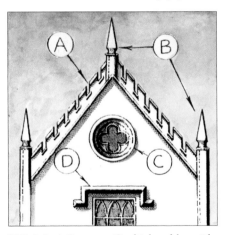

FIG 5.6: *A Regency Gothick gable, with characteristic stucco finish, stepped battlements (A), pinnacles (B), quatrefoil (C), and hood or drip moulding (D) above the window.*

roofs with end gables, pointed-arched windows, some with 'Y'-shaped tracery, drip mouldings above openings, tall Tudor-style chimneys, and a painted stucco finish.

Another popular form which peaked during the first half of the 19th century was the castle, a patriotic response to war with France or perhaps an owner's desire to re-assert one's social status in the subsequent period of worker and peasant discontent. The design had been inspired by romantic tales from the likes of Walter Scott and had been given acceptability by Robert Adam who believed that they were direct descendants of the architecture that the Romans had brought with them to these shores. Hence, they linked the Ancient World and Britain. Now alongside those castles which had survived the Civil War and had remained residences were erected new castles which, despite having the appearance of their medieval counterparts, can be told apart by the consistency of fine stonework throughout the building, a symmetrical façade and large windows neatly arranged in rows and columns. The castle remained an inspiration during the Victorian period and a variation called Scottish Baronial was popular. It developed north of the border and spread south after Queen Victoria acquired Balmoral in 1848. It is distinguished by tall outside walls surmounted by small corner turrets and round towers with steeply-pointed caps.

Foreign sources still influenced country houses, with a wider palette of styles now available to the architect. Italianate villas, featured in the

FIG 5.7: LOWTHER CASTLE, CUMBRIA: *At first glance it looks a very convincing castle, but look again and a house emerges. Note the central block has tall windows, with smaller square ones above, and pavilions at each end of the building, just like a Palladian mansion. The theatrical arrangement of towers in the centre, the perfect symmetry and the regularly-positioned windows confirm that it was built by Robert Smirke from 1806–11. The family moved out in the 1930s and it was partly demolished in 1957 leaving just the shell although partial restoration of the shell and the gardens is now underway.*

paintings which inspired the Picturesque movement with round towers off-set to one end, low pitched roofs and deep overhanging eaves, and arcades of arched openings, appeared in a few locations and inspired smaller urban residences. Napoleon's presence in Egypt had led to French archaeologists uncovering and making drawings of the great monuments they found. The Egyptian style which was inspired by these discoveries is characterised by thick round columns with lotus leaf capitals, walls which lean in at the top and large concave eaves, usually only details applied to a house or garden buildings. Increased

FIG 5.8: CRONKILL, SHROPSHIRE: *Its stark geometric shapes almost give it a 20th-century feel, but it was the creation of John Nash in 1802 and was inspired by the Italianate buildings in the pictures of the 17th-century artist Claude Lorrain.*

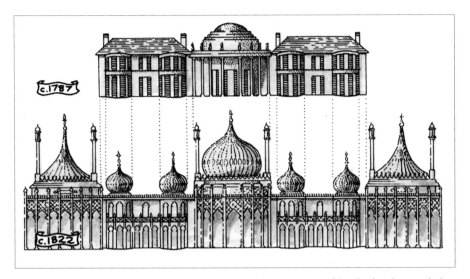

FIG 5.9: THE ROYAL PAVILION, SUSSEX: *This outrageous blend of Indian-styled elements was designed by John Nash for the Prince Regent from 1815–22. At its heart, though, is a far more conventional Neo Classical villa (the left-hand section of the top view) which was expanded for the supposedly bankrupt Prince and his lover Mrs Fitzherbert by adding the central dome and wing on the right in 1787. The dotted lines show its position within the Royal Pavilion's last incarnation.*

contact with India and China inspired a number of houses, most notably the Prince Regent's Royal Pavilion at Brighton. Its onion-shaped domes, exotic window and door styles, and chimneys disguised as minarets cover what was, until 1815, a modest Neo Classical house.

Despite becoming the chosen taste of the arch enemy Napoleon, Classical architecture was still prominent in country house design during this Regency period. The latest designs were influenced by the discoveries from Greece, and the temple which was seen as Ancient Greek architecture in its purest form features in part on many houses from this date. The main body of the house tends to be plain, with the roof hidden from view and a portico or colonnade projecting from the façade, with simple Greek Doric or Ionic columns and capitals.

Victorian and Edwardian Styles

From the 1830s, brick comes back into fashion. A wider range of materials allows the pitch and covering of roofs to vary according to style, and asymmetrically-placed towers appear, often used to house tanks which provided running water under pressure for new toilets and bathrooms. Now

FIG 5.10: SHUGBOROUGH HALL, STAFFORDSHIRE: *The garden front of this late 17th/18th-century house (see Fig 4.6) had the distinctive Regency, shallow-bowed central extension added between 1803–6 in a Neo Classical style. The delicate arched verandas either side of it are also characteristic of this period.*

with larger panes of glass available, the sash window could virtually dispense with glazing bars and give uninterrupted views across the owner's property. Later in the period large houses were built which hugged the landscape or were modestly set within woodland rather than dominating their surroundings. Timber-framing which since the 17th century had been unfashionable became popular again, sometimes just cladding, other times structural and usually set on top of a stone or brick lower storey and painted black and white (a largely Victorian fashion).

When Queen Victoria came to the throne there was intense religious debate centred on groups at Oxford, Cambridge and London as the Church of England faced up to an identity crisis. This in part had been caused by the Catholic Emancipation Act of 1829 which had removed most of the restrictions for practising Catholics dating back to the 16th century. One convert who rose to prominence at this time was Augustus Welby Northmore Pugin who, in a series of books, enthusiastically promoted Gothic architecture, based upon the accurate study of medieval buildings rather than the loose theme used in the earlier Gothick style. He argued that in order for buildings to have moral value they should not hide their function and structure and that they should use natural materials. This point of view had a dramatic influence upon

FIG 5.11: BULSTRODE PARK, BUCKINGHAMSHIRE: *The stocky Gothic tower in red brick is a typical mid Victorian feature. This muscular-looking building with an asymmetrical arrangement of spires, gables and battlements was built between 1861 and 1870.*

FIG 5.12: TYNTESFIELD, SOMERSET: *This extravaganza of Victorian Gothic Revival was built for William Gibbs from 1863 by architect, John Norton, with further additions made by Henry Woodyer and Arthur William Blomfield. It was purchased by the National Trust in 2002 after over £8 million was raised from the public in just 100 days, along with the largest single grant from the National Heritage Memorial Fund.*

Victorian architects. Pugin and others saw the Middle Ages, in particular the 14th century, as a time of high religious morality and the early buildings in this new Gothic Revival style use forms from this period for inspiration. There was no stucco hiding the materials used. Brick could once again be on show, with a preference for a rich red colour, with windows featuring pointed arches, tall slender towers and an asymmetrical layout being distinguishing features of early Gothic Revival houses.

From the 1850s to '70s there was a move to a more muscular form of Gothic, with dramatic decoration and stout towers, less influenced by the English Middle Ages and more by Continental sources. The most dis-

tinguishing feature of houses of this date is the use of polychromatic brick work where red or cream brick walls are broken by bands and patterns in lighter or darker colours.

Another popular inspirational source for country house building was the 16th century and early 17th century. Tudor red-brick houses and the imposing Elizabethan and Jacobean prodigy houses found fervent ground in this patriotic period (Fig 5.1). Even detail down to the strapwork decoration the Elizabethans so loved was copied, although the varying heights of windows depending on which floor the state rooms were in the original houses was usually not imitated.

Queen Victoria and Prince Albert had Osborne House built in the style of the

FIG 5.13: *Examples of 16th-century brickwork (top) and 19th-century (bottom). The sharper edges and finer pointing of the later example is one way of identifying Victorian houses from the originals they were based upon. The patterns formed by the exposed end (header) and side (stretcher) of each brick varied through the ages. English bond (top) featuring a row of headers then one of stretchers was common in the 16th and early 17th century. Flemish bond with a header followed by a stretcher on each row became the more popular from this point up until the late 19th century when English bond was revived.*

Italian Renaissance. It was inevitable that others would follow suit. Country houses and urban villas were designed in this Italianate style, with a peak of popularity in the 1850s and '60s. It was characterised by the use of tall, round-arched windows, with large panes of glass; towers with a series of narrow-arched openings along the top and a low pyramid roof; shallow pitched

FIG 5.14: BRODSWORTH HALL, SOUTH YORKSHIRE: *This mid Victorian Italianate house differs from earlier Classical styles in the mouldings around the windows, French doors, and two roughly equal height floors. Note there are no Classical columns on this façade as free-standing types were not favoured by Victorians, except on the portico across the entrance (right) which was a typical 19th-century feature.*

FIG 5.15: WADDESDON MANOR, BUCKINGHAMSHIRE: *A Victorian country house in the style of a French chateau, designed by the architect Destailleur. It was built in the 1880s for Baron Ferdinand de Rothschild, a member of a large Austrian banking family whose various relations purchased five other properties within Buckinghamshire because of its close proximity to London and the excellent hunting in the county.*

roofs with large overhangs supported on decorative brackets; and was usually executed in a light colour brick or stone. Larger houses inspired by the same Continental sources might have a symmetrical façade with parapets and vases.

A French style of architecture became popular during the second half of the 19th century due to the fashionable changes which were taking place in Paris under the reign of Napoleon III. This so-called Second Empire style is usually recognisable by the use of mansard roofs (which have a shallow top slope, followed by a steep lower one) and lines of dormer windows. These windows allowed rooms to be put into the usually limited roof void and made them popular in urban buildings where space was at a premium. Out in the country the chateaux with steeply-angled roofed towers and Baroque-type decoration also inspired a number of projects.

From the 1860s a new generation of architects began to find inspiration not in mighty medieval buildings but less imposing manor and farmhouses of the 16th and 17th centuries. Rather than designing strict copies, they used these sources to create new forms. They may at first seem similar to the originals, but on closer inspection their layout can be revolutionary and the details strikingly modern, especially in the hands of Arts and Crafts architects at the turn of the 20th century. Richard Norman Shaw was one of the leading designers in this Old English style who created country houses which no longer reached up to the sky and dominated their surroundings. They were more humble, low structures designed with the demands of the family taking precedence over the appearance of the exterior. Although they could feature the latest technology and modern materials, the façades presented the viewer with the impression that the buildings had grown progressively over centuries. They were characterised by long,

FIG 5.16: CRAGSIDE, NORTHUMBERLAND: *This dramatically-set mansion was designed by Richard Norman Shaw from the late 1860s, with inspiration coming from 16th-century manor houses, with timber-framed gables, mullion windows and tall chimneys. It was notable for being the first house to have electric lighting.*

sloping, tiled roofs overhanging low walls, with exaggerated tall brick chimneys, and mullioned windows filled with leaded glass which were often set in long rows tucked right up under the eaves.

As Norman Shaw turned his attention to developing new styles like the Queen Anne-style based upon the houses of the late 17th century with Dutch gables and white painted woodwork, (most timber was painted dark colours or grained to look like hardwood in this period), those who had been educated in his practice went out and developed the domestic revival styles further. The Arts and Crafts houses of the 1890s and early 1900s which they created used vernacular materials. This empowered skilled craftsmen to produce beautiful, quality fixtures and fittings, with the architect taking control of the whole project from the structure down to the handles on the doors. Most of the buildings produced by architects working under

FIG 5.17: WIGHTWICK MANOR, WEST MIDLANDS: *An Old English-styled house, asymmetrical, with a timber-framed exterior and Arts and Crafts interior. It does not tower over its site but spreads out with low-slung roofs, tall chimney stacks and an assortment of 16th-century window styles so appears to have evolved over time rather than having been erected in the 1880s and early '90s.*

FIG 5.18: STANDEN, SUSSEX:
Designed by Philip Webb in the early 1890s around an old farmhouse which had been purchased by a wealthy London solicitor James Beale, it not only retained elements of the original building but also used local materials and a form which suggested it had grown progressively over centuries.

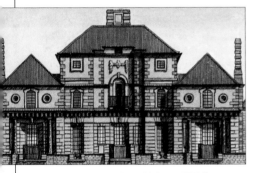

FIG 5.19: HEATHCOTE, LEEDS, YORKSHIRE: *This suburban villa designed by Sir Edwin Lutyens in 1906 combines the Arts and Crafts' use of local materials, with a variety of Classical sources to create a unique form of building characteristic of the great architect's later work. The form is Palladian (see Fig 4.14) but with late 17th-century, Baroque-style details and stone from quarries at nearby Guiseley and Morley.*

this banner were modest country houses or summer retreats, often incorporating an older building or feature which the architect now made a special point of preserving.

This was a time of great nostalgia. Traditional pastimes were revived, the National Trust was formed and *Country Life* magazine published for the first time. This magazine played a large part in promoting the designs of a young Sir Edwin Lutyens who, after producing some of the leading Old English-style houses, turned his attention to Classical styles. He used his unique skills to create new forms guided by the orders rather than direct copies of ancient buildings. The Edwardian period, in which the houses he created were most influential, is characterised by this mix of styles from Imperial classical buildings to recreations of Georgian houses, with symmetrical façades featuring distinctive low-arch tops to the sash windows.

The Layout of Houses

Despite an obsession with reviving the past, the layout of houses reflected the changing social climate and the demands of the new aristocracy. The piano nobile which dominated in the previous century was gone and the main rooms were now on the ground floor. The procession of state apartments became a thing of the past, with more informal rooms arranged in a less strictly symmetrical manner. Rooms were increasingly dedicated to a precise purpose in the 19th century, with morning, breakfast, smoking, music, and billiards rooms

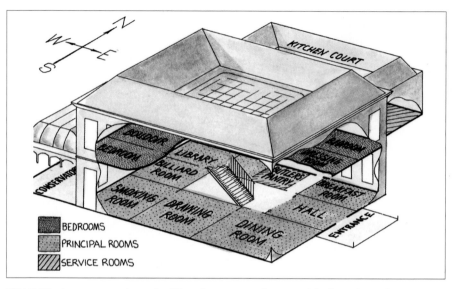

FIG 5.20: *A cut-away view of a Victorian country house, with the principal rooms now on the ground floor dedicated to a more precise use. Upstairs are the bedrooms and dressing rooms, while the service rooms are in the separate kitchen court at the rear. Note that the central stairwell is top lit by a glass ceiling light; these more imaginative illuminating effects are a feature of 19th-century houses.*

frequently appearing in the plan. In Arts and Crafts houses there was an emphasis upon the revival of the hall as a communal space. The careful control of light and the use of different levels of floor and height of ceiling made for innovative interiors. The awkward problem of where to site the service rooms was generally solved by building a courtyard or rear wing often to the north of the house. This meant the food was nearer to the dining room than it had been when sited in the 18th-century pavilions. With no restriction upon size, these service areas could incorporate the large number of specialist rooms required to service the ever-increasing demands of a Victorian country house.

The picturesque landscape gardens which appeared to draw right up to the house were by the Victorian period outdated. Now there was a return to terraces and flower beds which could be viewed from fashionable French doors and verandas. Exotic plants and trees from the furthest corners of the Empire were in vogue now that large glass conservatories and greenhouses had been developed. These were often built as a wing or even part of the structure of the house, a distinctive feature of 19th-century country houses.

Exterior Details

FIG 5.23: *A pointed arch formed out of brickwork above a sash window was a common way of integrating the Gothic style into a façade without compromising the practical rectangular shape of the window. The use of cream, grey and red bricks was popular in the 1860s and '70s as were bands of patterns and decorative crests on the roof.*

FIG 5.21: *Two Italianate-style windows with their distinctive Romanesque (semi circular) arches and large, single panes of glass with no glazing bars. Raised mouldings around the windows and decorative details above and within the arches often help to differentiate Victorian houses from earlier work.*

FIG 5.22: *An Italianate-style tower with arched openings, balustrade and urns. Another common design had triple arched openings with a flat pyramid roof, as popularised at Osborne House.*

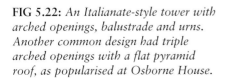

FIG 5.24: *Roofs on Gothic and Arts and Crafts houses were a prominent feature with gabled ends exposed and decorative bargeboards fitted under the eaves as in this beautifully-carved example from Wightwick Manor. Roofs were steeper pitched and could stretch down to the top of the ground floor (low-slung) on Arts and Crafts houses. Casement windows (side-hinged) were reintroduced in the late 19th century but usually have rectangular leaded lights, as in this example, rather than the diamond shapes widely used in the 16th century.*

FIG 5.25: *Arts and Crafts houses had plain mullioned windows in the bays, as featured here at Broadleys, Windermere, by C.F.A. Voysey. They were often tucked tight under the eaves of low-slung roofs. Shallow buttresses and deep overhanging eaves were also distinctive of this style.*

FIG 5.26: *Chimneys once again become a feature as architects were happy to expose the functional parts of the house rather than hide them behind a balustrade. Tall stacks copying Tudor styles were a key part of the design of many Old English and Arts and Crafts houses in the late 19th century, as here at Deanery Gardens, Sonning, by Sir Edwin Lutyens.*

The Demise of the Country House

On a sunny day in May 1869, upon a barren plain some 56 miles west of Ogden, Utah, USA, the final spike where two railroad tracks met was about to be driven home by Leland Stanford of the Central Pacific. His stroke with the hammer missed, but the eager telegrapher was already sending

FIG 5.27: EXEMPLAR HALL c.1900: *Some 40 years before this view is dated, the latest owner embarked on an expansion programme creating a wing to the right of the picture, with additional rooms for leisure and guest accommodation, a conservatory (left), a tower to hold the water tank and an enlarged service courtyard in the foreground. This was a time of great prosperity on the estate due to high agricultural returns, but by 1900 a sharp downturn in fortunes has resulted in the sale of much of the farm and parkland which is being swallowed up by new villas and terraces from the rapidly expanding nearby town (top).*

Unfortunately the situation would only get worse, Having lost the sole heir during the First World War and the aging lord of the manor shortly afterwards, the family's mounting debts and death duties forced it to sell Exemplar Hall and it became a private school. This was poorly run and by 1939 was in the hands of the armed forces as a training centre. At the end of the Second World War the council of the local town which by now had engulfed what was left of the estate purchased the site but the lack of maintenance had left the old hall unsafe and the majority of the building was demolished in the 1960s. Only the old kitchen courtyard was retained and has become offices while the remainder of the estate is now a public park. After all these years, only the church and its surrounding boundary have survived from the original scene in 1400.

THE ENGLISH COUNTRY HOUSE EXPLAINED

the message that the first trans-continental railway across America was complete. Now huge quantities of grain and livestock from the west could be moved east by train and then, aided by breakthroughs in refrigeration, shipped abroad. Back in England, landowners sitting in their country houses were basking in the warm glow of a golden age in farming. They were oblivious to the fact that, by the mid 1870s, American imports were keeping the price of corn steady and in the following decade lowering it. The agricultural depression triggered by these imports and the effects of a general economic downturn, meant reduced rents and income for the aristocracy. They were also affected by a loss of power as most males received the vote and were hit by increased bills from the introduction of death duties in 1894, and higher rates of income and super tax in 1909.

Many houses had already been sold off or left empty before the First World War. Worse was to come, however, especially for those families who lost male heirs in the conflict and could not pay the tax demands and bills in the tight economic climate after the war. During the 20th century these huge buildings designed for a more affluent generation became a drain on the upper classes. Large numbers became schools, hotels and offices, or were partially or completely demolished (Fig 5.7), only surviving today in the name of an estate which was often built over, swallowed up by rapidly expanding suburbs as happened at Exemplar Hall.

Thankfully, many country houses

FIG 5.28: CASTLE DROGO, DEVON:
Completed in 1930 and then on a much reduced scale from Lutyen's original grand scheme, this modern interpretation of a castle is often regarded as the last great country house and marks the end of the age of aristocratic rule.

have survived although often only through diversification into other fields like theme and wildlife parks, museums, and as locations for special or corporate events. Some still remain in the same family, others maintained by bodies like the National Trust and English Heritage. If you take what was once the six Rothschild houses around Aylesbury in Buckinghamshire (Fig 5.15) as an example, they are now an RAF camp, a hotel, a religious centre, an out of bounds school, with the two remaining ones open to the public through the National Trust. None of them remain in the family's hands.

SECTION II

THE COUNTRY HOUSE IN DETAIL

CHAPTER 6

Interior Structures

❖

🌸 Panelling, Ceilings and Fireplaces 🌸

FIG 6.1: *A Victorian interior with labels of the key elements of the room which can be found in other periods.*

If the exterior of a country house was prone to occasional tinkering by new owners, then the interior was susceptible to what could be regular and complete makeovers. An Elizabethan house might still retain its original façade despite some new trimmings and the odd extension but inside the rooms could be a medley of later Baroque, Rococo, Neo Classical or Victorian Gothic styles. What was once the saloon could now be a picture gallery while a withdrawing room could later house a billiard table. The interior was personal and could be more opulent, exotic and outrageous than the public exterior of the house, with each owner stamping his or her personality and demands upon it. However, underneath these unique and individual features there are some general structural changes and fashionable fixtures which the recognition and dating of can help one to unravel and better understand the development of a country house and how it would have appeared when originally decorated.

Walls

Medieval interiors were not the cold spaces we often see today. Originally they would have been colourful, with whitewashed or painted walls decorated with patterns, text or lines simulating masonry. Wall hangings usually made of cloth painted in strong colours were used to reduce draughts, especially at the lord's end of the hall. Tapestries were a luxury of the very rich and only appear in country houses from the 14th century. By the Tudor period, wood panelling covering the lower part or complete height of the wall became fashionable. It was composed of frames with moulding around the edges except along the bottom where it was chamfered to make it easier to clean and with square

FIG 6.3: *Small square panels from the late 16th century (top), with moulding around the top and sides (A), a flat chamfer along the bottom (B) and, in the finest examples, strapwork decoration (C). By the late 17th century large panels with classical proportions (bottom) could incorporate panelled doors and bolection moulded fireplaces.*

FIG 6.2: *An example of linen-fold panelling which was popular in the late 15th and early 16th centuries.*

panels inserted. Earlier ones had distinctive linen fold patterns or decorative carvings, whilst later ones were more usually just fielded (raised in the centre with chamfered edges). During the 17th century, the proportions of wooden panelling changed, with each wall of the finest rooms often divided into a lower section (the dado), a main body and then a short upper frieze, decorated with pilasters and classical motifs. In Restoration houses, carving reached breathtaking delicacy in the hands of craftsmen like Grinling Gibbons, with intricate patterns of naturalistic fruits, flowers and swags framing or decorating panels.

By this time, though, plastering the wall which helped reduce the fire risk was becoming fashionable. The plaster was made from lime or gypsum, often with hair, straw or reed within to give it strength. This was then applied over wooden lathes (thin strips of wood) which had been pinned to the wall. The surface was punctuated by mouldings made from plaster, stucco or even paper maché, which formed classically-proportioned panels, cornices and

FIG 6.4: *A section of wall showing how the plaster was applied to the lathes, projecting out of the left-hand side, and then built up in layers before the moulding was applied.*

decorative pieces, with wooden dado rails and skirtings to protect it from the backs of chairs which were positioned around the edge of the room at this date.

Where decoration was applied, flamboyant Baroque shapes were still acceptable even in later Palladian houses. By the mid 18th century a new variation known as Rococo (from the French word *rocaille* which described the rocky encrustations which featured on the fashionable grottos of the time) was popular. This was distinguished by deep, flamboyant, naturalistic forms like shells set in asymmetrical patterns and often painted in white and gold. In the second half of the 18th century, architects like Robert Adam, who created his own interior design style, were influenced by new Greek, Roman and Etruscan discoveries, and flatter, more delicate mouldings, with swags, vases, griffins and gold beads decorating panels which were painted in more subdued pastel colours.

Fabrics like silk damasks and leather were used as wall coverings and usually pinned to wooden battens to fix them in place. Wallpapers were first introduced from China in the 17th

Honeysuckle Paterae Husks

FIG 6.5: *Adam-style mouldings and details reflecting the latest Greek taste.*

century though they were not glued to the surface as modern versions are. Flock paper made from left-over wool sprinkled on glued pattern areas of the paper featured in some 18th-century houses while French papers, with exotic scenes or simulated fabric patterns, were still popular into the Victorian period. In later Georgian houses, principal rooms could feature arched recesses or curved alcoves for a statue or have completely round rooms with a dome above based on examples from the Ancient World. Pairs or rows of columns could also be introduced for added grandeur and to control the proportions of a room.

By the 19th century it had become fashionable for furniture to be scattered around the room, with tables and chairs arranged in intimate circles rather than up against the sides of the room. As a result, walls with a full height of hanging paper or fabric and without the protective dado rail appear, although the rail and panels still remained acceptable in certain rooms. The more refined and pale patterned papers and fabrics of the Regency home gave way to strong colours and bold designs in the Victorian Gothic home; this in turn giving way to less intrusive two dimensional designs, lighter colours and a revival of oak panelling in later Arts and Crafts houses.

FIG 6.6: *Early Georgian wallpapers (top row) copied floral and patterned fabrics, many inspired by Chinese designs. In the Regency period, stripes and Adam-style papers were popular (centre row). By the Victorian era, richly-coloured, three-dimensional papers were common (bottom left); in the second half of the century, lighter, simplified and often two-dimensional designs grew in popularity (bottom right).*

Ceilings

Ceilings did not exist in most medieval halls as the central hearth necessitated the roof being opened to the rafters although the trusses which supported it could be lavishly carved and colourfully decorated. The introduction of the chimney on a side wall permitted the owner to insert a room above and therefore a ceiling which could have exposed moulded beams, joists and decorative bosses at their junctions.

FIG 6.7: *A beamed ceiling, in effect the main bridging beams and joists supporting the floor above, which, as in this example, could be moulded and have decorative bosses fitted across the junctions.*

Wooden panels were fitted between to make a flush surface which could be painted. By Elizabethan times, a timber roof could be decorated with raised plaster geometric patterns. By the late 17th century, skilled plasterers were creating Classical-style ceilings, with large oval or rectangular centrepieces featuring paintings surrounded by delicate flowers and swags. In Palladian houses, architects endeavoured to create room spaces which would form a single or double cube. As pleasing to the eye as these proportions would have been, the immensely tall walls would have left paintings and decorations too high to be viewed. So, large concave coving (coffered ceilings) were used so they could be displayed in the new lower wall space below. In late 18th-century Adam interiors, the plaster moulding became flatter and more delicate. Pale colours were introduced to highlight the designs, with combinations of pinks and greens, blues and reds, and green, yellow and black often used. Domes and flat barrel-shaped ceilings were also popular with the Neo Classical designers. In the 19th century skylights of

FIG 6.8: *Examples of a late 16th-century plaster ceiling (left) with deep geometric pattern, a late 17th-century one (centre), with a painted scene within the oval, and a late 18th-century one (right), with colour highlighting the shallow plasterwork.*

FIG 6.9: *A section of Rococo-style ceiling which has been restored to its former glory in white and gold at the parish church which stands alongside Witley Court, Worcestershire.*

iron and glass created new lighting effects, especially over stairwells, while a central flower or medallion moulding from which a chandelier could be hung also became popular; while later Arts and Crafts designers re-introduced beamed ceilings.

Floors

The original ground floors of most medieval houses would have been of compounded earth made by raking the surface, flooding it with water and then beating it with paddles when dry. Additives like lime, sand, bone chips, clay and bulls' blood could also be used for strength or appearance. By the 16th and 17th centuries these rooms could be expected to be covered in stone slabs or perhaps the Dutch fashion of black and white marble tiles. Bricks and clay floor tiles were becoming common in

the south and east, with the earliest ones being generally larger and unglazed (glazed versions appear in the 18th century).

In the Georgian period the grandest rooms would have polished stone or marble floors, with brick vaulting below to support the weight now that basements were common. Other floors were composed of boards with early planks wider, or of irregular width, and butted up against each other; thinner regular-sized boards with tongue and grooves only appear in the 19th century. Hardwood boards were polished, cheaper softwood ones painted or grained to appear like a better quality wood, then most of the surface was covered by rugs, carpets or floor cloths. Parquet wood patterns were popular in the early 18th century and were revived again by Arts and Crafts designers.

FIG 6.10: *Parquet flooring often laid in a herringbone pattern as in this example was frequently used in earlier houses and was revived by Arts and Crafts designers in the late 19th century.*

Carpets first appeared in the 17th century as pieces laid in the centre of the room. Fully-fitted versions made by sewing sections together on site were used in some of the finest rooms from the mid Georgian period but smaller movable pieces which were easier to clean remained common until the 20th century. In the late 18th century as one person increasingly controlled the interior design scheme, an order would be placed for the carpet to be woven into a pattern to match the ceiling design.

In Victorian houses the wider range of architectural styles and greater specialisation of rooms results in a broad range of surfaces from contrasting stone or marble squares to medieval patterned floor tiles. New encaustic tiles with coloured patterns based on medieval designs were popular in Gothic houses, with plain unglazed ones in terracotta, black or buff used in service rooms and areas of heavy use.

Fireplaces

In the great medieval hall, the smoke from the central fire escaped usually through a louvre (French for *opening*) in the apex of the roof and was often left burning overnight with a pottery colander called a couvre-feu (French for a *fire cover* from which we get the word *curfew*) placed over it. The first improvements came with a screen which trapped the smoke from a hearth at one end of the room, or a large hood often made of timber and daub which hung over a fire along the wall, until finally the fireplace and chimney developed. In these early examples, the term 'chimney' (derived from the Greek word *kaminor* meaning 'oven') applied to the whole fireplace and stack

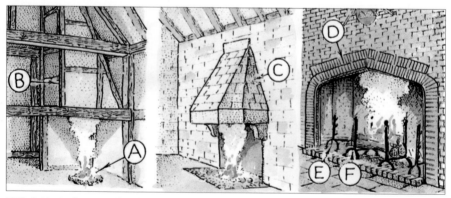

FIG 6.11: *In later medieval halls, the hearth could be moved in a corner (A) and a section above panelled to form a smoke bay (B) to channel the smoke up, while another alternative was a smoke hood (C). By the Tudor period recessed fireplaces behind a four-centred arch (D) or a lintel was fashionable with cob irons (E) which supported the spits on which food was roasted, while the logs were held in place by the fire dogs (F).*

FIG 6.12: *A late 16th-century, four-centred, arched opening, with a decorative over mantel above.*

together. The surround or chimney piece was typically a wide, flat-arched opening in Tudor houses, which was required to fit a large log-burning fire. During the 16th century coal from the north-east (shipped to London and hence known as sea coal) became available to the rich and later fireplaces became smaller as this new fuel could produce the same heat in a more compact lump. Unfortunately for the men who used to climb up the chimney to clean it, these new types were too small, so from this period on, young boys were used.

By the late 16th century the fireplace had developed into a principal feature in a room and was lavishly decorated with an ornamental over mantel above it. In the late 17th century a more restrained type of surround with bolection moulding (raised further off the wall near the centre) was set within the panelling. During the 18th century, stone or marble types with a shelf above and Classical columns or figures up the sides were popular, with broader mantels and the latest in Neo Classical motifs in the later Georgian period. By the 19th century, coal was widely available and more efficient register grates with decorative tiles up each side were common from the 1870s. Arts and Crafts architects often preferred log fires and reintroduced them into inglenook fireplaces or created wide

FIG 6.13: *A late 17th-century fireplace surround with distinctive bolection moulding all the way around the opening.*

FIG 6.14: *A late 18th-century chimney piece designed by Robert Adam. His examples are often distinguished by human figures (caryatids) in place of columns at each side and by a plaque with a raised decorative scene in the middle. Rather than the firedogs which held logs, the now smaller opening features a fire grate which holds coal in a compact block to increase combustion.*

FIG 6.15: *A distinctive Arts and Crafts-style fireplace with wooden over mantel and surround featuring glass cupboards, shelves and seating.*

surrounds featuring shelving and glass cupboards painted white with bright green and blue tiles.

Doors

Early doors were made from vertical planks of wood fixed by nails to horizontal beams, and held onto the surround by iron hinges or pins. These and their more decorative variants may have sufficed in a Tudor manor but the Renaissance gentleman and his descendants demanded something to fit in with their classical decoration. Panelled doors thus developed. Early ones had just two panels but by the 18th century the familiar six-panel

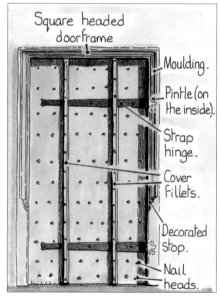

Square headed doorframe

Moulding.

Pintle (on the inside).

Strap hinge.

Cover fillets.

Decorated stop.

Nail heads.

FIG 6.16: *A late medieval or Tudor door composed of vertical planks with horizontal battens on the other side. These doors closed onto the back of the wall or frame.*

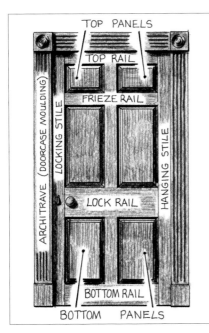

FIG 6.17: *A Regency six-panelled door, with labels of its parts. The concentric circles or bulls' eyes in the top corners are distinctive of this period.*

design was common. Not only were these doors elegant but they were also lighter, so smaller butt hinges could be used which could be concealed out of sight between door and frame. Woods like mahogany and oak were left exposed, but if cheaper softwoods like pine were used they would always be painted. This same rule applied to any other wood panelling or carving in the room. Victorians tended to use four-panelled designs with the later revival of old English styles seeing a return to plank and batten doors with highly decorative iron strap hinges.

After the Restoration, the surrounds which had been part of the structure with moulded and carved sides and tops became lavish door-cases embellished with columns and Baroque decoration with entablatures and a pediment across the top. Sometimes a double set of doors was fitted, usually to help keep food odours out of adjoining rooms; while the famous green baize door which separated the main house from the service rooms had the material pinned to one side to keep offensive noises at bay.

Stairs

The earliest way of ascending to what few upper rooms there were in a medieval house was by stairs which were little more than a sturdy ladder or, in a more impressive stone building, a narrow spiral staircase. As rooms on upper floors gained importance, wider and more elaborate stairs were required to reach them, often in a separate tower or short extension at the rear. By the early 17th century the more familiar closed string staircase was becoming popular, with separate treads and risers running into a side string course which was supported on thick corner and end posts called newels. They were considered a great status symbol and their oak posts and balusters were beautifully decorated, often displaying coats of arms with carvings of beasts and, later, classical figures and naturalistic details. Their importance could be further emphasised by being built in a separate room often at the end of the hall, a few examples still having carved dog gates at the bottom which were

FIG 6.18: *An early 17th-century closed string staircase, (where the treads and risers run into the side support), with decorative balusters (A) and newel post (B), with a dog gate at the top.*

FIG 6.19: *Regency cast-iron balusters which rest upon the treads (open string).*

FIG 6.20: *A late 17th-century balustrade, with rich wooden carving.*

used to keep the animals in the hall at night.

As joinery techniques improved, the newel posts ceased to rest on the floor and the steps appeared to float up the staircase (although they were actually cantilevered off the wall). Some had their now exposed undersides plastered like a ceiling, with decorative mouldings and even pictures; while others had beautiful parquet floors fitted on the landings and elaborate carved posts. During the 18th century staircases have open strings with the now more elegant and thinner balusters (often set in pairs or threes) resting directly on the tread; cast-iron types with mahogany handrails and spiral ends being very distinctive of the later Georgian period. Victorian staircases reflected the style of the house with replicas of a past age common; only Arts and Crafts designers made new inventive forms which heralded in the modern styles of the 20th century.

CHAPTER 7

The Upstairs Rooms

❖ Halls, Drawing and Dining Rooms ❖

FIG 7.1: BLACKWELL ARTS AND CRAFTS HOUSE, WINDERMERE, CUMBRIA:
The medieval hall, Tudor farmhouse parlour and Victorian billiards room are combined here in one by Hugh Mackay Baillie Scott. He, along with other Arts and Crafts architects, reinvented the hall, making it once again the social centre of the house after it had been relegated to a glorified passage in the Georgian period; an example of how the role and importance of the principal rooms of the house could change over the centuries.

The rooms within the main body of the house could be divided into those for reception and entertaining or for the private use of the family. As the priority for most owners was to impress their guests, it is the former group which tend to be the most lavish and fashionable. The degree of splendour within these principal rooms would reflect the wealth of the owner and how close he was to Court and political life. The more private ones reflected the owner's personal taste and daily requirements although since guests may have been received in these family rooms at some point they would still have a degree of class. With the constant redecorating and building in the most fashionable houses, these rooms may have changed not only in appearance but also in the role for which they were originally designed. Although the furnishings will usually reflect the taste of the last or current owner, there are characteristics like the position of the room within a house, the size and proportions of the space and the type of fittings used which can help identify its original use and how it may have once appeared.

FIG 7.2: *A view of a late medieval hall, with the lord's end on the right and the buttery and pantry accessed through the doors on the left.*

The Hall

The hall in the early medieval period was the centre of life for the household – a large open space in which the lord of the manor, his fellow nobles, personal army and servants would eat, drink and sleep. It was where local justice could be administered, farmland managed, men gathered with arms and guests were entertained. It was the heart of the community, where all classes were accepted. In the middle of this tall space would have been a hearth with the fumes from the fire drifting up through a gap in the roof, with at one end a raised platform called the dais on which the lord sat, often with a large window illuminating it, and the other a screen which helped keep out the draughts from the main entrance.

Sleeping with a group of belching servants, snoring soldiers and scratching dogs, upon filthy and muck-ridden straw somehow lost its appeal to later medieval gentry! They built a wing onto their hall to create private rooms at one end and sometimes a buttery and pantry, with a passage between to access the separate kitchen at the other end. The later Middle Ages were also a time of great social changes accelerated by the Black Death, which saw the breakdown of the old feudal system and the renting out of manor lands, such that the decisions on managing the fields were increasingly made by the new yeoman farmers. Therefore the hall's role as the centre of the estate and community began to fade. By the 16th century, in most country houses, the hearth was being moved to the side of the room, ceilings inserted and a great chamber created above, with the old space below becoming a servants' hall. However, in

Private chambers

Open hall

Dais

Screens passage

Service rooms

Great chamber

Inserted floor

Hall

Fireplace

FIG 7.3: *Two views of the same medieval hall before (top) and after a fireplace and upper floor have been inserted (bottom) in the 16th century.*

some houses, the large communal room lasted well into the following century.

As Elizabethan gentlemen were erecting new houses for display, they usually incorporated a large hall in the centre of the house running lengthways across it when viewed from the front. For the first time, though, at Hardwick Hall, it was turned ninety degrees and became the long, thin entrance room we associate it with today. As guests would now pass through this space, servants eating and sleeping within it was no longer acceptable, so separate accommodation out of sight was provided. In this period the hall would usually be panelled with a new, patterned, plaster ceiling in the finest houses, with a beautifully-carved staircase by which guests could ascend to the principal rooms separated off at one end. By the 18th century it had risen in importance again, forming part of the piano nobile, with external steps leading up to it. They were often of a refined classical style with columns, alcoves, pale plastered walls and a floor of light-coloured stone or marble. These cool rooms were also used for dining in the heat of summer, as well as being spacious enough to welcome a party of guests or to serve as an anti chamber. Although the hall fell from prominence during the 19th century, its original form was revived in Arts and Crafts houses where architects keen to replicate its medieval communal role formed large open spaces with inglenook fireplaces, galleries and seating where guests could be received, meet before dinner and be entertained afterwards.

FIG 7.4: KEDLESTON HALL, DERBYSHIRE: *In the 18th century, fantastic marble and stone halls were a feature of Palladian houses. This example by Robert Adam has fluted columns, arched niches containing sculptures and a huge coffered ceiling above.*

The Great Chamber

One of the first rooms to appear when the owner sought more privacy was an upper chamber in which he could dine and sleep called the solar (from *solarium* with the root *sol*, meaning 'sun'). Food was brought up in a procession from the service rooms at the other end of the hall, past his household sitting along tables in the hall and then up a staircase at the side of the dais. By the later Middle Ages, though, the lord was likely to be receiving guests here and eating in state so, with its increased status, the room became more lavishly decorated with a separate bed chamber leading off it.

What was now referred to as the great chamber was popular during the 16th and early 17th centuries. It could usually be found upstairs in a cross wing or built directly above the hall when this was divided horizontally by inserting a ceiling. It was used as a showroom for hanging tapestries or family portraits, for important meals and even for music, plays and dancing. Wood panelling was fitted to the walls and horsehair covers put on chairs as they did not retain the smell of meals eaten within (although most people still sat on benches and stools at this date); while details like royal coats of arms above the chimneypiece and themes like hunting depicted in the decoration were popular. Later great chambers started to increase in scale, with coved ceilings, paintings built in above the chimneypiece and richly-carved decorations showing fruit, flowers and birds.

The Banqueting Hall

Once guests had finished their main course they could retire to a separate room to eat a luxurious selection of wafers and spices which, in the 16th century, was referred to as a banquet. In some larger houses an impressive banqueting hall was built specifically for this role, either as a stand-alone building in the garden, a room within the house with access to the outside, or in some cases built on top of the roof so the relaxing diners could admire the views.

The Parlour

Great chambers and banqueting halls became too excessive for everyday meals, so a parlour would have been provided for the family. Parlour comes from the French verb *parler*, meaning 'to speak', which reflects its other role as somewhere to hold private conversation. The parlour can be found in country houses from the 15th century and was usually simply decorated, with a gate-leg table which could be removed after meals. It had little other furniture as masses of plates and cutlery were not used at this date. Guests brought their own knife and spoon (forks were not in general use until the 18th century). Larger houses may have had more than one, perhaps

FIG 7.5: *Banquets could be held in modest halls within the house, as well as in large banqueting houses set in the garden as in this example at the former Campden House, Chipping Campden, Oxfordshire.*

a great and little parlour, while in 18th- and 19th-century houses these private family rooms were often called morning or breakfast rooms, with the parlour becoming a common feature in middle-class housing.

The Dining Room

By the 18th century, the great chamber was replaced by two rooms: the saloon and the dining room. The latter was used for important meals and became a major element in country houses where it was as much for show as for eating. Walls were usually plastered or stuccoed with floral, fruit and animal designs around the cornice and friezes, while shutters were recommended in place of curtains as they did not retain the odour of food. It was a masculine space, with strong colours used mainly to set off the gilt-framed paintings which guests could admire and discuss. The gate-leg table and chairs could be pushed up against a wall when the meal was over as rooms were still rather flexible in their role at this date.

Victorians were better at ergonomics than their predecessors and would rather receive their meals hot, so the dining room would not be positioned too far from the kitchen. A serving area would be nearby where the different courses that made up the meal were collected before they were brought into the room. Some dining rooms even had hidden doorways so that servants could emerge to remove dishes with minimal fuss. It was only at the beginning of the 19th century that the table became a

FIG 7.7: CALKE ABBEY, DERBYSHIRE: *This dining room created in 1794 is decorated with delicate plaster mouldings framing small inset pictures, while the alcove behind the columns features a sideboard which could be used when serving meals. Note the door just behind the right-hand column which could give servants discreet access to the room.*

fixed piece of furniture in the middle of what was now a permanent dining room, with ladies retiring after meals and the gentlemen left to fill it full of smoke and drunken laughter.

The Saloon

The saloon (a French word derived from the Italian *sala* meaning 'a hall') was used for entertainment and display. In Baroque and Palladian houses it tends to be on the central axis behind the entrance hall, with the dining room and drawing room on each side and views over the garden to the rear. This great room was regarded as essential in 18th-century houses and would be as tall as the hall; even if this meant lifting the floor of the room above if it was

FIG 7.6: *A mid-Georgian dining room, with distinctive strong-coloured walls to act as an effective background to the gilt-framed paintings hanging on its walls.*

being fitted into an existing suite of rooms. As one of the great showrooms, the architect could make use of its grand scale and produce round or double-cubed spaces with alcoves, apses, imposing coffered or domed ceilings and shallow bowed windows looking out across the gardens.

It was here that the best pieces of artwork, sculpture and furniture could be displayed, while concerts, balls and other entertainment were held within. As the room was not used for dining, wall coverings of delicate fabrics could be used and paintings hung upon them. By the 19th century many saloons had become no more than picture galleries and were referred to as such, becoming more of a museum now that dances and great gatherings would take place in the ballroom. Glass panels were often fitted in the ceiling to cast more light on the collections on display.

The Drawing Room

As the medieval solar developed into the more luxurious great chamber, a separate bedroom was usually built off it for the owner. Between these rooms an ante chamber was supplied where the owner could take a private meal in the days before a parlour and his servant could sleep on a straw pallet and guard the door to his bedroom; a small space which was referred to as a withdrawing room.

By the late 16th and early 17th centuries this had become more of a private sitting room where the owner could keep his favourite or most valuable pieces of art. In Baroque houses, though, it formed part of the state apartments and was nearly always positioned between the saloon and the bedchambers, becoming an intimate room, often with a lower ceiling than the saloon and hall, with delicate

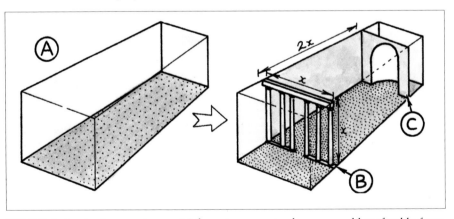

FIG 7.8: *Important rooms in new 18th-century country houses would preferably form a single or double cube. However, when refitting an existing house, moving walls to create these proportions was not usually practical. At Syon House, London, Robert Adam was faced with a long thin room (A), so he inserted a screen of columns (B) and an apse (C), thus making the space between them a double cube.*

FIG 7.9: *A Georgian drawing room, with a lighter colour scheme than the dining room and a less formal appearance. Small tables for playing games, especially cards, were very popular.*

fabrics on the walls and curtains with pelmets around the windows (before it became fashionable to hang them in all rooms). It was regarded as a feminine space. While the men smoked and drank back in the dining room, the ladies would withdraw to what was now generally referred to as the drawing room. Its role was vague – you could find card tables, spinning wheels or a piano within, with music often being the theme of the decoration. Throughout the Regency period the informality grew, with chairs grouped around the room rather than up against the walls. The French fashion for hanging a mirror above the fireplace

became popular and there was increased comfort and luxury, with upholstered sofas and large draped pelmets gathered above the curtains. It retained its feminine role throughout the 19th century, always with lighter decoration and a feminine touch. In many houses it became the finest or best-positioned room.

Bedchambers

As owners sought greater privacy during the 16th century, so a separate bedchamber became common. Although it could shut the owner off from his household at night, it was still a public room in which friends and

FIG 7.10: *A bedchamber, with a rail closing off the alcove containing the four-poster bed and a doorway to the left of it giving access to a private sleeping room. (Rails were only a short-lived fashion and rarely survive today).*

guests could be received. The four-poster bed was the dominant and single most expensive piece of furniture in the house; its curtains keeping out draughts and providing privacy from servants. It was usually positioned on the opposite side of the room from the window which had a dressing table on the wall between. The owner would dress, wash and bathe in this room although by the late 17th century a separate space for this was provided and the old dressing table became more of a showpiece.

In the large Baroque houses of this date the state bedchamber was at the end of the enfilade after the saloon and withdrawing rooms, although it was less ornate than those which preceded it. There was also a fashion for positioning the four-poster behind rails or within an alcove divided off from the rest of the room by columns which helped keep the room clear for other

uses during the day. It made a grand climax to the procession of retiring to the state bed (although there may have been a hidden door to the side of the alcove for the occupant to access another more private bed after the ceremony).

In the 19th century, as the principal rooms began to be sited on the ground floor, the bedrooms moved upstairs, although it was usual to retain a bedchamber on the ground floor for infirm or elderly members of the family. These new rooms tended to be smaller than the old state bedchambers but more numerous as the Victorian gentleman was likely to be entertaining large parties of guests rather than smaller family groups.

Dressing rooms

By the late 17th century, a separate dressing room was usually provided off the bedroom. The gentlemen's version was known as a cabinet. It was where William III met his closest circle of ministers; the word 'cabinet' still refers to the senior ministers in a government today. Corner fireplaces, oriental artwork and small pictures were popular in these rooms as they tended to have lower ceilings than the bedroom. In the late 18th century a lady's version known as a boudoir (from the French verb *bouder*, meaning 'to sulk') was popular. It was a private sitting room where the lady could sew or read in increasing luxury. As bedchambers moved upstairs and became the conventional bedroom, the male cabinets next to them were known simply as dressing rooms.

Another small room off the bed-chamber or dressing room was the closet, a room for keeping the close stool (basically a chamber pot covered by a hinged top). In earlier medieval houses a chamber pot would have been used in the great chamber by the owner, while the rest of the household used separate garderobes which were tiny rooms often in a tall extension with a simple hole in a board to form a toilet seat and with either earth below which could afterwards be used as fertilizer or with a drop down directly into the moat. In 16th-century country houses a separate closet could hold the close stool and may have been no more than a cupboard-sized room with no light or ventilation. This was bad enough for the dignitary who had to use it, but even worse for the poor servant who had to walk through the house with a pot full of effluent afterwards. By the later 17th century, the closet had become more of a private sanctuary, a larger room where the owner could expect to be seated on something more luxurious like veneered wood or even a velvet seat, until the development of flushing toilets from the late 18th century made closets a thing of the past.

The Long Gallery

Elizabethans were well aware of the limitations of the English weather and built themselves huge long rooms, illuminated by masses of glass windows, which they could use for recreation. These long galleries were in high fashion for a relatively short period from the mid 16th to mid 17th century; yet their distinctive long, thin

FIG 7.11: LITTLE MORETON HALL, CHESHIRE: *A garderobe extension which protrudes from the front of the building; something which would never be accepted on a later house. The right-hand picture shows the interior of one of the garderobe closets, with the hole leading directly down into the moat.*

form is a notable feature of numerous country houses even after later alterations. They can be more than 150 ft in length, have at least two walls full of glass, with wood panelling elsewhere and a long boarded floor on which people could promenade, whilst enjoying the views. They were used by all the family for sports like real tennis, games, including billiards or shove halfpenny on long shuffleboards, and even for work outs on early dumb bells or exercise chairs. Other long galleries were more educational, with portraits of important dignitaries lining one of the long walls and symbols with hidden meanings in the plasterwork. Their shape, however, did not fit easily into the later Baroque houses and although some were built in the 18th century for

FIG 7.12: LITTLE MORETON HALL, CHESHIRE: *This spectacular long gallery is perched on top of the south wing (see Fig 1.1). Real tennis was probably played here as two early 17th-century balls were discovered behind the panelling.*

In fact, early libraries, which at the time were very much a male preserve, can often be found built off the closet. In the Georgian period, collecting books was a fashion inspired by an intellectual thirst for art and politics. Thus, the importance of literature elevated the library to a state room, increasingly used by all the family as a place for letter-writing, playing cards or as a meeting place for guests. Open bookcases became popular from the mid 1700s, replacing earlier glass cabinets, while the awakening of interest in English history and literature later in the century inspired a fashion for Gothic-styled libraries.

artwork, dances and after-dinner chats, many of the existing ones became libraries or picture galleries. By the Victorian period their role, as was usual, had been taken over by numerous smaller rooms, with the children now playing in the nursery, male recreation in the billiards room, the ladies using their boudoir or drawing room, topical discussions held in the study and dancing taking place in the ballroom.

Library

The Renaissance gentleman educated in the Humanities may have started gathering books but these precious items would not be kept in one particular place until the 17th century. His collection was usually stored in the closet (keeping a book or newspaper in the toilet today is not such a new idea!).

FIG 7.13: *Early bookcases usually had glass doors to protect the precious contents.*

Chapel

The importance of religion in daily life in medieval England meant that it would be unthinkable not to have a chapel or church, and usually both, for the lord and his household in which to worship. The private chapel was used for daily prayers while the parish church next door would be attended by the owner, his family and household every Sunday. In larger houses the chapel would usually have a comfortable gallery above for the lord and his family which could be accessed from their private apartments, while the household could use the main body of the room below. Chapels that survive today are often in the earliest part of a house, as very few new ones were built after the Reformation of the 1530s, although many had a later Classical refit.

The situation, though, was very different for the Catholics who especially after persecution in the wake of the Spanish Armada had to practise their religion in secrecy. It was from this date and into the 17th century that priest holes were built into the homes of practising Catholics, with their sons sent abroad to become priests and then returning as secret missionaries, often basing themselves at remote homes of staunch supporters. Ingenious hiding places were thus required for when the dreaded pursuivants (priest hunters) came knocking and many country houses still have hidden passages or secret chambers today. By the late 18th century, as anti-Popish feelings died

FIG 7.14: BADDESLEY CLINTON, WARWICKSHIRE: *This sacristy, a room off the chapel where the vestments and sacred vessels were stored, has an innocent-looking box with a cross upon it on the far wall. This, however, covers a secret passage leading to a priest hole which was used when the house was raided in 1591. The Catholic preachers may have hesitated though if they had realised the hole they were dropping down was previously the garderobe shaft!*

down, Catholics were permitted to have a chapel, perhaps just a converted room, but it was not allowed to be visible as such from the outside. It was not until the Catholic Emancipation Act of 1829 that they could once again build new chapels and churches.

CHAPTER 8

The Downstairs Rooms

◆

▦ Kitchens, Scullery and Dairy ▦

FIG 8.1: *One corner of an early 19th-century kitchen in the basement of a country house, with an adjustable open range (left), dresser and table being the main components of this key service room.*

It was one thing to excite guests with architectural magnificence and lavish decoration, but the country house owner would also have to satisfy their stomachs in order to leave them with a positive impression of his or her hospitality. Medieval lords are known to have spent anything from half to three quarters of their entire income on food and drink. Even in Victorian mansions, vast sums were spent on maintaining specialist staff and buildings for taking the raw ingredients produced on the estate in at one end and supplying a wide variety of exotic meals at the other. The fittings and

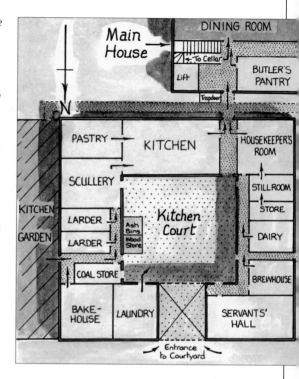

FIG 8.2: *An arrangement of service rooms around a kitchen courtyard of a 19th-century country house, with arrows showing the direction by which ingredients, food and then the finished meals could reach the dining room. The Victorians were the first to plan the layout of the service rooms with a real understanding of ergonomics. The rooms were carefully arranged to make the production process smooth while the butler's pantry and housekeeper's room were located where an eye could be kept on precious commodities, as well as on the staff.*

layout of most service rooms which survive in country houses today date from this period. By the turn of the 20th century, food and domestic supplies were increasingly coming from a local wholesaler and hence there was less need for areas to process raw ingredients, and many service areas became redundant or were converted to other uses.

The status and mix of people who manned these rooms also changed over the centuries. The strict hierarchical structure of discreet servants, dressed in black and white uniforms who would never speak directly to their employer is a rather late development and far removed from earlier arrangements. The medieval household was an all male community ranging from knights down to local peasants who would serve their lord but also eat and drink at his table. The move towards greater privacy gradually broke up this arrangement and by the 18th century the engine room of a country house was composed of male and female servants, with a wider range of specialist rooms covering all aspects of storage, production, cooking and cleaning. It was only in the Victorian houses that the structure of servants strictly adhering to the rules and regulations with which we are familiar from watching period dramas on television reached its zenith.

The Kitchen

The most important room around which the other service rooms were arranged was the kitchen. Its position in relation to the country house was mainly dependant on a constant battle with fire safety and the removal of the odours produced in cooking. It was a smelly, noisy and dangerous place and not every lord therefore wanted it right next to his dining room. The earliest kitchens in medieval houses were timber-framed or stone structures, often square in plan, with pointed roofs and a louvre opening at the top. They were separate buildings in order to reduce the risk of burning down the main hall if the kitchen went up in flames. The food was brought from here along a covered way, into the house via the kitchen passage, through the hall and up to the dais or private chamber for the lord, after which the household were served.

By the Tudor period, though, the kitchen was often part of the main house, typically one of the rooms around the courtyard or within the service end of the hall. Walls might be lime-washed plaster, with floors of stone or brick covered in straw or rushes. A hearth set in a wide fireplace was used for roasting meat; baking ovens with arched openings were built into the wall nearby; and there would have been a charcoal stove on which delicate dishes like sauces could be simmered. Some had a separate boiling house with a large copper in which

stews, stock and meats could be boiled. Although there would be a table for preparation, there was limited other furniture since there were few cooking utensils and implements to store.

In the 17th century, the division which opened up between the polite and service sides of the country house saw the kitchen increasingly moved into the basement to keep the servants out of sight of the family and guests above. Some of the kitchens had stone-vaulted ceilings above which helped reduce the fire risk while open ranges with raised, iron fire baskets, holding the increasingly available coal rather than wood, first appeared. In later

FIG 8.3: STANTON HARCOURT MANOR, OXFORDSHIRE: *One of the few remaining medieval kitchens in the country which had a covered passage (a pentize) leading to the hall and parlours, with louvres just below the conical roof to let out the smoke.*

Palladian houses the kitchen was on the move again, this time out of the way in a separate pavilion or wing although many of the male-dominated areas like the butlers' and stewards' rooms and the precious beer and wine cellars remained below the main house. Some still had large hearths, but most featured ever more elaborate roasting ranges with mechanical spits and hob areas to the sides. Walls were sometimes painted blue as it was believed to repel flies. The huge kitchens with masses of strange and elaborate devices which feature on country house tours today are usually a product of the 19th century. In the early Victorian period it became difficult to retain staff as many villagers went off to work in the factories, so the lady of the house became increasingly involved in the running of the kitchen. This prompted many to improve the standards below stairs or build better-

FIG 8.4: *This 17th-century kitchen had the fire (A) contained within the metal fire dogs cooking the food supported on cob irons (B) and the spit (C). A clockwork mechanism spins the wheel (D) at the end of the spit though at this date most were probably turned by young boys. The fat dripping from the joints is caught in a tray below (E); other food is heated in pots hanging from the rail (F) and spare spits are stored above the fire (G). In the corner is a baking oven (H) and a stove (I), with fuel stored in the recesses below (J), while the gaps (K) above allowed air in to feed the charcoals held on round grid irons above (like a modern barbecue). Pots were held above the heat on metal trivets or from a crane (L) allowing the food to be cooked gently. A feature of country house kitchens which appears in all periods is the large central table (M) on which the meals were prepared.*

FIG 8.5: *A Victorian kitchen with a closed range built into an old fireplace on the left and an open range retained on the far wall, with a spit in front turned by a smoke jack. The kitchen was the engine room of the house which along with other service rooms was focused upon providing the family and guests with a conveyor belt of delicious and exciting food and all the trappings they would expect to accompany the meals.*

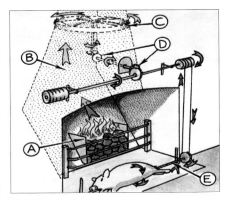

FIG 8.6: *A diagram of a roasting range and smoke jack, with the stippled area showing the workings within the chimney. The sides (A) of the range were adjustable and controlled the size of the fire. The spit in front of it was turned by the smoke jack which was powered by smoke rising up the flue (B) spinning the fan (C) above, and turning the connecting shafts and gears (D) which, via a horizontal rod above the fireplace and a pulley at the end, spun the spit (E) below.*

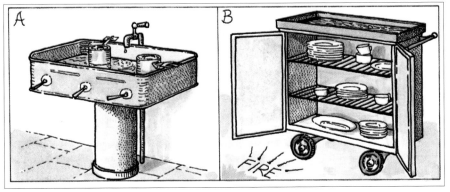

FIG 8.7: *(A) A bain marie which was a shallow sink filled with hot water designed to cook sauces or keep them warm. The copper pots within had tags on the handles to identify the contents. (B) A warming trolley with metal-lined doors which was wheeled in front of the fire to heat the crockery within and at the same time protected the servants working behind from the immense heat which the ranges emitted.*

designed service courtyards to the rear or side of the house featuring new cast-iron ranges, running water, better ventilation and numerous time-saving gadgets which were designed to make life easier and more hygienic.

Walls were still lime-washed, white or yellow now, with glazed white wall tiles covering areas behind the sink, the range and sometimes the remaining walls up to a certain height. The room was often tall, with windows high up or in the ceiling, with rods to open them and ventilate the room. Dressers stored the now massive assortment of utensils and pans, known as the batterie de cuisine (originally meaning copper and brass ware which was battered into

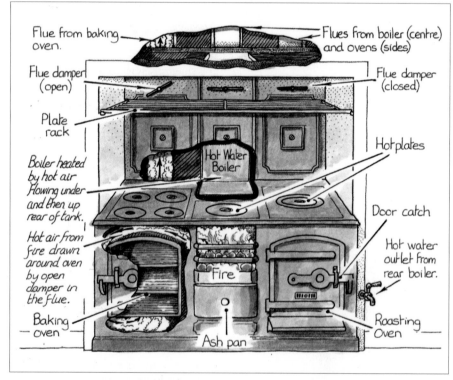

FIG 8.8: *A 19th-century closed range, with labels of its key parts. These had developed from the late 18th century when an iron baking oven was placed to one side of the old adjustable fire and a boiler placed on the other. In the Victorian period more efficient closed ranges became popular in which the central fire had an iron plate above it and the hot fumes were forced out around the ovens either side rather than wasted straight up the chimney. Circular hobs on top of the range gave a gentle heat for simmering (replacing the old stove) or could have the iron centre part removed to give a more intense heat and a hot water boiler was built in behind the fire.*

shape), along with numerous strange-shaped moulds because the Victorians loved jellies. New technologies start to appear in the kitchen like steam cooking as boilers could supply it under pressure to kettles containing food or warming cupboards. The centre of the kitchen was usually dominated by a large wooden table, often made of deal, for preparing the meals, with slatted boards around for servants to stand upon.

FIG 8.10: *A 19th-century knife polisher into which abrasive powder was poured through a hole at the top. The knives were then inserted into the slots next to it and when the handle turned, it rotated felt pads which polished the blades within.*

FIG 8.9: *A free-standing roaster was placed in front of the open section of a range, with a clockwork mechanism at the top which turned the meat while the heat reflecting on the curved back cooked it.*

Bakehouse, Pastry and Stillroom

In larger houses separate rooms were provided for some types of cooking or preparation. One of these was the bakehouse where bread, cakes, and biscuits were produced. It was ideally in a separate block or at least as far from the house as possible so that the flour dust and oven odours would not penetrate indoors, and to make deliveries of food stuffs and fuel easier. The earliest ovens were brick and beehive-shaped, with a small arched opening and may have taken a number of days to reach the correct temperature. They proved to be better at baking than the cast-iron ovens which were introduced

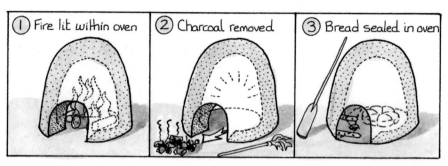

FIG 8.11: *The beehive-shaped oven was first filled with wood, coal or a local fuel and heated up to temperature. The charcoal or ash was then removed and the bread put in before the door was sealed for baking. Later brick types had a distinctive arched door set into the wall, usually to the side of the fire.*

with 19th-century ranges, and many survived into the 20th century. The room would also contain floor chests, benches with a trough for kneading the dough, and a sink for washing utensils like the peel (the wooden paddle used to lift the bread in and out of the oven).

A few larger houses had a pastry room which originally was where meat pies and pastries were made, although by the 19th century it was used for the production of confectionery, sweets and tarts. These rooms are often found on the cool northern side of the service block, with the oven in an adjoining room in order to keep the temperature down. The room would contain shelves and pin racks, benches with marble tops for rolling pastry, and bins below for flour.

The stillroom was originally used for the production of perfumes, medicines and cordial waters which were made from flowers, herbs and spices. This was an important room in medieval and Tudor households, usually being run by the lady of the house. By the late 17th century it was sited in the basement and, as the aristocracy would never be seen there, the housekeeper took charge and it was often located next to her room. Polishes, waxes and soaps could be produced here but these, along with distilling, died out during the 18th century as it became easier to buy in the products. In the 19th century it was mainly used for making preserves, pickles and desserts, and for storing ingredients and preparing light meals.

Dairy

The dairy was rare among the service rooms in that it could be lavishly designed and decorated. Originally this was due to the involvement of the lady of the house who, up to the 19th century, could be found running its production of unadulterated milk, butter, cheese, etc. By the late 18th century, however, the gentleman of the house became interested in all forms of

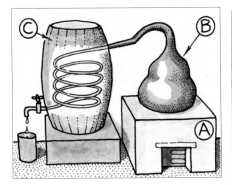

FIG 8.12: *A diagram showing 19th-century distilling equipment which could be used to produce cordial waters. The furnace (A) heated up a mix of flower petals or herbs in liquid within the bottom of the still (B) and the steam rose up and along the thin tube, condensing in the spiral within the worm tub (C) which was full of cold water.*

FIG 8.13: *A view showing how hygienic and yet ornamental some dairies had become by the late 18th and early 19th century. The fountain in the middle emitted a spray to help keep the temperature down; while skimming dishes, pans, vases and churns stand upon the low stone table around the perimeter.*

agricultural improvement and the application of science to farm production, including the dairy. The room then became one with white tiled walls, a marble floor and shelves, and in some a central fountain to cool the room. The milk was poured into shallow pans and tubs, then skimmers removed the cream which settled on top. This was either stored in vases or churned in tubs to make butter and cheese. Heated pipes would help keep the temperature steady in winter at 50–55 degrees, while there would usually be a cleaning area or a separate scullery next door for washing the utensils, pans and dishes. In some houses the dairy work was carried out in the scullery, with the dairy itself just being used for storage, a role it increasingly played during the 19th century as more products were bought in from outside rather than made on site.

Brewhouse

Another important production room was the brewhouse. In the days before safe drinking water became available, beer was drunk at mealtimes, including at breakfast. The brewhouse was tall in order to fit the coppers within, and was usually distinguished by louvre openings high up for ventilation. It would be positioned to provide as easy access as possible for the deliveries of malt and hops to the trap door and chute which led to the beer cellar under the house. The beer produced varied in strength depending on its intended use, with small or table beer made from the weaker wort produced in the final third mash and consumed as we would soft

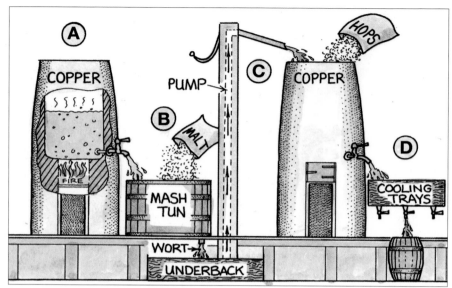

FIG 8.14: *A diagram of the basic brewing process: (A) Water is heated to just below boiling point in a large copper, with a fire beneath the tank and a doorway below this from which to remove the ashes. (B) The water is poured into the mash tun and malt added to produce wort which is poured into the underback below. (C) The wort is pumped up into either the original copper or, as in this example, into a second one and is boiled up with hops. (D) The final mixture is run off into cooling trays and then into casks for storage.*

drinks today. A medium strength brew called ale was made from the second mash, while a strong ale or malt liquor was produced by adding extra malt into the first mash. This latter brew was usually for special occasions like the birth of an heir, when the ale was bottled and then stored until his coming of age celebrations.

Scullery

The scullery (derived from the Latin word *scutella* meaning 'a salver or dish') was where plates and dishes were washed. In the country house it was more versatile and many of the messy tasks like peeling, chopping and washing vegetables, preparing meat for roasting and gutting fish were done here and hence it is usually found next to the kitchen. The sinks would preferably be under the window so those washing up had the best light in which to make sure the crockery and utensils were clean. Early sinks were carved out of stone or made from wood lined with lead. By the 19th century, earthenware or china sinks with wooden draining boards to the sides and plate racks above were common. In the days before centrally heated water was available, a separate boiler or one built into a range was essential, with the latter also useful for some cooking tasks. There would have also been a pump for cold water until a tank mounted in a tower enabled it to be supplied under the pressure of gravity to taps protruding out of the wall above the sink.

Buttery and Pantry

The word 'buttery' is of French origin, and comes from the same source as 'butt' and 'bottle'. It was where the casks of beer and other drinks were stored while they were being dispensed. Long-term storage would usually be in the cellar or outbuilding. The word 'pantry' is derived from *panis*, the Latin for bread, and was originally where the grain and bread were kept. It was thus usually sited at the service end of the medieval hall so these staple parts of the meal could be easily distributed. The pantry was the responsibility of the pantler, while the buttery was the responsibility of the butler. Although the latter name survived, the buttery itself faded from use, its role being taken over by the butler's pantry. This is not to be confused with the pantry which still appears in later houses and was used for the storage of dairy products and some cooked dishes, as well as bread, though in Victorian houses it was often called the dry larder.

Larders and cellars

The larder (from the Latin *lardum* meaning 'bacon') was originally an

FIG 8.15: *A copper set in a corner of a scullery. Water was heated in the circular tank held within a brick or stone frame.*

outbuilding where the raw meat was salted and stored. By the 19th century there would be a number of them for specific uses: the wet larder was the one where pieces of meat were prepared and stored (it was called a butchery if whole carcases were brought in); the dry larder had a similar role to the pantry; while fish and bacon larders are self-explanatory. Game larders were often a separate round or octagonal structure where deer and birds were hung but by the late 19th century when shoots could bag thousands of game birds at a time, larger rooms were required, some with primitive forms of refrigeration. The larder had to be cool and so is often found on the north of the building. If not, it had overhanging eaves or plants shading its walls, while wet cloth might be thrown over the roof in the hottest of weather. Windows could be part- or fully-covered in gauze

FIG 8.16: *An old wooden octagonal game larder set in the shade of trees just behind the service block of a country house.*

to permit a through draught and to keep out insects. Around the white-washed or tiled walls would be slate, brick or marble shelves, with hooks in the roof for hanging meat and perhaps an ice box for fish and cold dishes. Cellars were also used for the long-term storage of beers and wines and, later, for the huge quantities of coal which were required.

Servants' rooms

As the owner separated himself from his staff and they, in turn, became wage-earning servants of a general, lower status, a separate servants' hall was provided. This meant that they could eat their meals among the service rooms, out of sight of the lord and his guests and not cluttering up his splendid new marble and stone entrance hall. Sometimes called the common hall, these rooms were provided with a long table and, in some, a little beer barrel on wheels which could run up and down it for the dispensing of drinks. Although the senior servants would dine with the rest of the staff, they would usually retire to one of their private rooms. The butler's pantry was usually in the main house, close to the dining room so that the butler could take charge of serving the food, but also with convenient access to the cellars and the main entrance. Within could be found the containers of drink, table linen, crockery, cutlery, and glasses which were in regular use, plus materials to clean them and perhaps a brick safe in which the more precious pieces would be stored. As it

FIG 8.17: *A feature of fish larders, before the days of refrigerators, was an ice box which was used for storing fish and cold dishes. Ice from the estate's ice house was put into the compartment at the side which cooled the lead-lined interior.*

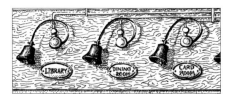

FIG 8.18: *A line of bells would have hung near to the butler's pantry to tell him in which room service was required. The bells were connected by wires in tubes to each room. Previously, servants had to sit and wait to be summoned by hand-held bells.*

FIG 8.19: *A shallow stone sink and pump, with various pieces of equipment used in washing which could be found in the laundry or washroom.*

was also his office and living room, a table, chairs, wash-basin, fireplace and a bed could be found crammed into what was often only a 12 x12 ft room!

It was only from the later 17th century that women started to take a significant role within the country house and the housekeeper first appears. Her accommodation was usually positioned near the service rooms where she could keep an eye on the staff, and with a door leading directly into the stillroom. The bulk of the crockery could be stored here on shelves (later ones with glass fronts) or in a separate china store close by, and also the table linen which she was responsible for cleaning and repairing. Again, as it was an office and sitting room, there would be similar contents to the butler's pantry. Most houses would have a steward who was responsible for the running of the estate, and he would usually have been provided with his own room, while the cook would generally use the housekeeper's room for office work.

Laundry

The laundry or washroom originally had a large copper for boiling clothes and a pump to bring in water, while the wet washing was often simply draped over hedges and lawns to dry. Later houses would often have two rooms: a wet laundry where the washing took place with boilers providing hot water and a vent in the roof to let the steam out; and the dry laundry where the airing, ironing and folding took place. This would contain drying racks suspended from the ceiling, a range or stove on which the irons could be heated and a large table which would have been covered with sheeting when in use. The centre of the room was often dominated by a box mangle, a large, flat-bed trough which, when filled with stones, pressed down onto a bed below and flattened the partially dry linen in between.

CHAPTER 9

The Gardens and Estate

❈ Terraces, Parks and Gatehouses ❈

FIG 9.1: LAMBETH PALACE, LONDON: *The gatehouse was often the most important building after the main hall in a medieval and Tudor country house. It not only displayed the owner's power and wealth but also housed a senior member of the household in its upper rooms. It is just one of the buildings which can be found today around the main house which were once vital parts of the gardens and estate.*

The Gardens

There is evidence that gardens were laid out within the grounds of medieval castles and country houses. Some were small areas for growing herbs and flowers, or for playing games and relaxing, while others were possibly larger in scale. During the 16th and early 17th century, as the country house developed from an inward-looking defensive building to an outgoing display of wealth, gardens became an important part of the design. They were a place of leisure, with games, plays and masques acted out upon their lawns, and contemplative walks taken through flower beds and arbours. Knot gardens, with geometric patterns formed from low box hedging (some designs reflecting the Elizabethans' love of secret symbols), were popular, as well as sundials, brightly-painted statues and a raised walkway or a large mount for viewing the scheme (look for a grassed-over mound up against the edge of a garden today). Mazes were often laid out although at this date they were formed from low hedges which the viewer could see over; the tall hedged maze, correctly termed a labyrinth, was a later development.

During the Restoration, the returning Royalists brought with them new ideas on gardens from France, with rectangular beds of low hedging containing flowers and coloured gravels called parterres (a French word meaning 'on the ground') spread out from the house on a much larger scale than the previous knot gardens. Terraces with balustrades, long rectangular water features with cascades and fountains, and topiary cut into geometric shapes were among the features to be found. With the accession to the throne of William and Mary in 1688, Dutch gardens became fashionable; usually smaller than their French counterparts, with more elaborate detailing, trees in tubs, lead statues and a mania for tulips! Many shrubs were grown purely for their foliage and were known as greens, being brought inside in winter to the greenhouse which, at this date, was a conventional building, often with

FIG 9.2: *The rear of an Elizabethan country house, with a knot garden in the foreground, a maze behind that, a banqueting house (rear left) and a mount (rear right) from which the scheme could be admired.*

FIG 9.3: POWIS CASTLE, POWYS: *A view from the terrace, with its balustrades and statues, over this late 17th-century garden. The plain lawn to the right originally contained parterres, geometric-shaped ponds with fountains, statues and a cascade flowing down from the now densely-wooded wilderness beyond (far right).*

accommodation above for the gardener. The value of light to plant growth was not appreciated at this date.

The gardens also began to spread out into the estate, with arrangements of high clipped hedges in geometric patterns called a wilderness laid out for walking within, although where this name survives today the area tends to be more appropriately natural and wooded.

During the 18th century, the landscape garden was developed. It was inspired by 17th-century paintings of classical scenes featuring expanses of lawn, lakes, ruined castles, towers and temples. The garden designers who transferred these images to the English countryside were increasingly professional men, the most famous of whom was Lancelot 'Capability' Brown, who gained the name 'Capability' from his habit of informing clients that their gardens had capabilities. In order to create these vast expanses of private parkland, the owner would remove

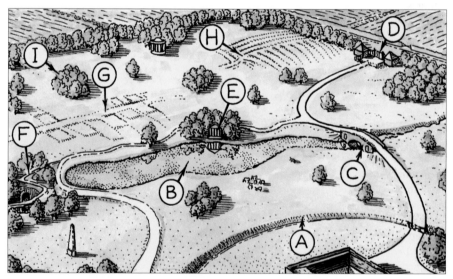

FIG 9.4: *An aerial view of an 18th-century landscape garden, with labels highlighting some of the features to look out for today. The house is near the bottom right corner and is surrounded by a ha ha (A). In the middle distance is a serpentine lake (B), formed by damming the local stream, which is crossed by a classical-styled bridge (C), carrying the main drive from the similarly treated gate lodges (D). From the drive, visitors can view the various eye-catching buildings, including a mock temple (E) overlooking the lake or wander down to the grotto (F), formed around the waterfall created on the dam. Traces of the old village (G) and the ridge and furrows of the open fields (H) which were moved when the garden was created can still be seen in the form of lumps and bumps in the open grass which is punctuated by clumps or individual mature trees (I).*

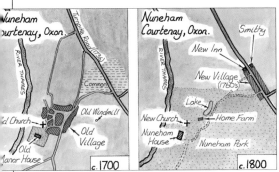

FIG 9.5: *Maps of Nuneham Courtney, south of Oxford, showing the original village (in red) next to the manor house in 1700 and the re-sited settlement a century later built alongside the new turnpike road to make way for the new Nuneham House and its landscape park.*

villages and turn over fields. The dispossessed locals may have been housed in a new village, well out of view of the house, but many were simply evicted and moved to the towns to find work in the new factories and mills. The land they left behind was transformed into gently rolling parkland, interspersed with clumps of trees and large serpentine lakes (in a long, curving shape like that of a serpent) and bounded by a thick band of trees. Despite these subsequent changes, the faint banks and ditches which marked the original homes and fields can still be seen in many parks today.

The 17th-century formal garden was designed to be viewed on foot from fixed points, with straight avenues leading the eye into the distance. The landscape garden, however, was to be appreciated by guests arriving in carriages, so clumps of trees and eye-catching follies were arranged so that the view slowly changed to reveal distant objects as visitors were driven along the winding road. With a growing appreciation of nature and the picturesque in the second half of the 18th century, ruined garden features, grottos, shell-lined caves, and furniture and buildings made from bark-covered wood became popular. The park also came right up to the front door although this meant that the deer and livestock could wander up to the house,

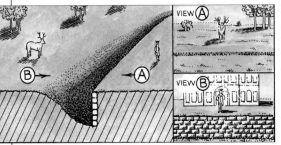

FIG 9.6: *A section through a ha ha, designed so the owner looking out would see view (A) where the ditch is virtually invisible, giving unbroken views over the park, while the deer looking towards the house would see view (B), with a wall preventing it getting closer to the house.*

too. Therefore, a ha ha was devised, (a ditch with a vertical wall one side and a slope the other), to stop the animals getting too close.

By the turn of the 19th century the aristocracy were becoming bored with the plain expanses of green. A new breed of designers like Henry Repton reintroduced formal beds of flowers, gravel walkways and terraces around the house, while thicker blocks of trees with greater variety were laid out in the park. These schemes were often smaller than the preceding landscapes so, in order that the owner would appear to have a larger park, eye-catching features were erected on distant higher ground. These remote towers and obelisks can often be found today many miles from the house from which they were intended to be viewed.

Victorian gardens were inspired by a variety of historic and exotic sources but were often compartmentalised. Different areas could be given over to formal planting, water features, scenes from distant lands, or woodland. Priority was given to the content rather than the structure of the design, with plants and trees laid out in such a way that the individual plant would be displayed at its best rather than for any collective effect. Shrubs and trees from all around the globe could now be nurtured in glasshouses before being planted out, especially conifers which, along with rhododendrons, formed distinctive dark barriers around country houses. Some trees and shrubs were planted to make arboretums; if only conifers were grown they were known as pinetums. Rock and wild gardens, shrubberies and ferneries were also popular towards the end of the century.

FIG 9.7: BIDDULPH GRANGE, STAFFORDSHIRE: *A restored Victorian garden laid out in compartments, with differing themes linked by serpentine paths and tunnels, and characterised by exotic trees, rocky outcrops and structures inspired by buildings from around the globe.*

In the 20th century the expense of running a large team of gardeners proved too much for many owners. Land was either left to grow wild, often becoming overgrown with rhododendrons, or was sold off for farming or building, with the occasional mature tree or garden feature appearing in modern housing estates. Several of those gardens which have survived to the present day have now been restored to their original form or as near as possible to how they might have once appeared.

Orangeries and conservatories

In the late 17th century there was a fashion for growing orange trees in pots. Orangeries were constructed to protect the trees in winter, with the additional benefit that the buildings could be used for social functions in summer when the pots were placed outside. These early types were often built into a terrace with just a row of windows exposed at the front; later ones were built off a wall or might be free-standing. They were typically brick or stone structures, with a tiled roof and a row of south-facing windows set within a line of archways (a loggia), although some had glass roofs inserted later when they were used to store exotic plants all year round.

Conservatories became a distinctive feature of 19th-century gardens. They were built onto the house, with large metal frames often cast with decorative arches and with vast areas of glass to house plants from around the Empire. Hot water heating systems were used, while heat might also be obtained from a fireplace and flue on the other side of the rear wall. The high maintenance these required meant that many were abandoned or removed in the 20th century.

Follies, monuments and grottos

There have always been garden structures within which to socialize, contemplate or appreciate the surrounding flora. In the 16th and 17th centuries there were banqueting houses where diners could retire after a meal and enjoy sweets (see Fig 7.5), and

FIG 9.8: TATTON PARK, CHESHIRE: *This conservatory was designed in 1818 but unlike most later versions, it was a free-standing stone and glass structure and still holds exotic greenery today.*

gazebos or summer houses from which they could admire the owner's clever garden designs and discuss their hidden meanings. It was in the 18th century, though, that the strange, monumental and exotic structures which we term as follies were built as part of the landscape gardens. They were not as useless as the title implies, though. They acted as eye-catching features and as venues for garden parties, music recitals and social meetings.

Although the main house had to be built with strict rules and fashions in mind, architects were given a much freer range with garden structures. Some were copies of the round towers which featured in the paintings of artists like Claude which had inspired the landscape garden in the first place. Others were copies of Roman and later Greek temples, triumphant arches and

FIG 9.9: *A selection of follies ranging from (clockwise from top left) Classical temples, Egyptian buildings, Chinese pagodas, and Gothick structures (which looked nothing like genuine medieval buildings). These exotic styles were often considered too daring for the main house but were happily used in the garden. The finest collection in their original setting is probably at Stowe Landscape Gardens, Bucks.*

rotundas, pieces of the Ancient World recreated for the owner fresh back from his Grand Tour. Gothic architecture appears on the country estate in the mid 1700s, a generation or two before it would be considered suitable for the main house. With a growing appreciation of nature and all thing British in the late 18th century, sham castles, ruined structures and fake prehistoric stone circles were erected. Another source of inspiration was the exotic Far East, with Chinese pagodas and bridges proving especially popular. Statues and monuments also featured in these park

schemes and it is not unusual to find an impressive stone pinnacle erected to the memory of a favourite pet. In the 19th century, compartmentalised garden buildings from a historic period or distant land added the signature to a garden theme.

Lakes, fountains and bridges

Moats which surrounded late medieval manor houses were probably part display and part fishpond (freshwater fish was a vital food source). Few were ever built to keep an army at bay. In the finest 17th-century gardens, long rectangular ponds, often referred to as canals, were a distinctive feature. Some came with complicated water schemes to supply fountains within them and cascades at the far end. In the 18th century, huge lakes were built as part of landscape gardens. They were usually formed by building a dam across an existing stream and flooding the bottom of the valley. To carry the main road up to the house, ornamental bridges were built. Often designed by leading architects, they were usually beautifully proportioned Classical structures with round or segmental arches, balustrades and niches, and carefully positioned to fit in with the overall scheme.

The Estate

The estate was the foundation upon which all country houses were built. It

FIG 9.11: WITLEY COURT, WORCESTERSHIRE: *Fountains could be designed with huge jets of water but none so tall as this restored example. Most were powered by gravity, with a tank or lake on higher ground feeding water down pipes to a small outlet which focused the jet.*

FIG 9.10: STOWE LANDSCAPE GARDENS, BUCKINGHAMSHIRE: *Classical-styled stone bridges were a distinctive feature of landscape gardens and were often designed by leading architects rather than engineers. This Palladian-style bridge was a popular form in the mid 18th century.*

not only provided the owner with financial income but supplied the house with food, materials and manpower, making it relatively self-sufficient even up to the 20th century. These estates are most likely to have been formed in the general reorganisation of land ownership which took place after the Norman Conquest, although some estate boundaries can date back much further. During the feudal medieval period the majority of them operated as manors, run by the lord (or his tenant in chief if the lord resided at another estate), from a castle or principal house (manor house). The estates would comprise a demesne, land on which the produce grown was for the lord's table only, which the villagers would have to send a family member to work, as well as supply a certain amount of produce from their own fields. The remainder of the fields were used by the villagers, with decisions on how it would be farmed made at the manor house which, in addition to its role as local court house and close proximity to the parish church, made it the centre of the community.

Famine and then the Black Death in the 14th century played their part in breaking up this system. Unable to find peasants to farm their fields the lord of the manor granted the land to a new breed of individuals in return for rent. Thus, the feudal peasants slowly became tenant farmers and the gentry became landlords. The manor house would still be fed by produce from its own land, although as the landscape was reorganised by enclosures from the 15th to 19th century a home farm was usually established from which it would be managed. The village which housed the staff working the estate was often moved or rebuilt during the Georgian and Victorian period, principally so that the approach to the house would complement the grand building and also so the owner could keep a tight rein on who lived there.

Stables and Coach Houses
Every country house would have had stables close by in which were housed saddle horses, coach horses and cart horses, together with their foals. Most date from the 17th to the 19th century and are usually found with a large archway featuring a cupola and clock above which leads into a courtyard

housing the stables, coach houses, blacksmiths, joiners and a tack room, the latter having a fireplace to keep the leather warm and access up to a hay loft. Coaches had become popular with all levels of the gentry by the late 17th century, and most would have two, a basic one for everyday use and another of greater luxury.

Hunting and Racing
Hunting was the favourite pastime of medieval lords of the manor and most established deer parks near their house in which to contain the animals. These

FIG 9.12: DUNHAM MASSEY, CHESHIRE: *This stable block (used as a coach house) with its distinctive white cupola dates from the 1720s and originally contained a brewhouse, a bakehouse and a large space for the carriage horses (riding horses, cart horses and dairy cows were kept in a separate block).*

were usually roughly circular enclosures of up to 200 acres surrounded by a ditch and bank, with a fence along the top from which the deer could be released at the time of a hunt. As this form of hunting declined in popularity during the 17th century so the old deer parks were often turned over to agriculture although their distinctive round shape can often still be spotted on maps today.

The fox had become the quarry of choice by the 18th century, bringing together all ranks of the estate with the

FIG 9.13: *The old ditches surrounding deer parks can sometimes still be found. They differ from those which kept livestock out of old woods which would have a bank on the inside edge (top). Because they were designed to keep the deer within the enclosure, the bank was on the outer edge (bottom). These features will be much reduced in height today.*

master, usually the lord himself, leading the pack, a huntsman responsible for looking after the hounds and hunt servants to organise the event. Developments in gun making meant that from the late 17th century shooting replaced hawking and by the 19th century had become the preferred sport of the aristocracy.

All these activities would have left some mark on the estate. For instance, there would be kennels for the pack (usually on one of the estate farms) and strips of wooded land often labelled as coverts in which foxes and game birds could be protected before the hunt or shoot. Another popular pastime in the 18th century was horse racing and there may even be a circular or oval track marked on old estate maps.

Home Farms

The fashion for nobles to become involved in agricultural improvement from the 18th century produced a spate of new farm building, featuring the latest technologies. By the mid 19th century, the home farm of the estate had become more like an efficient factory production line rather than a rustic collection of barns. It would ideally be formed around a courtyard, with brick or stone buildings containing some of the earliest farm machines At first these were powered by a horse wheel (look for a round or polygonal structure on the side of the farm in which the animal walked round), a water or wind mill, and later by a steam engine, the chimney of which often survives today. Other buildings on these model farms could have contained cattle stalls, stables, store rooms, poultry houses, cart sheds, and sometimes a dairy. The brewhouse and bakehouse might also be here rather than in the service rooms; often next to each other as the same skilled man was required for both processes. Outside there would be a house for the bailiff, steward or manager, from which an eye could be kept on the farm-hands' comings and goings.

Dovecotes

Another essential feature of the estate which provided the owner of the house with a more diverse assortment of food, especially in winter, was the dovecote. This was a round or square structure with a pointed roof and openings in the gables from which the birds could fly out. Inside, the pigeons (doves were not kept as they won't return home) nested in recesses, with a ladder for servants to gain access to them. Although some early examples do survive, most of those which you will find today date from the 17th to 19th century.

Fishponds and Warrens

A set of ponds in which fish were reared for the lord's table was an essential feature of any medieval house, usually often in the form of a row of roughly triangular pools tiered one above another. Although most were later abandoned or filled in as sea fish became more widely available, some were incorporated within later garden schemes and their distinctive shape can still be identified or spotted as dried out indentations on the ground. The medieval estate would also provide the

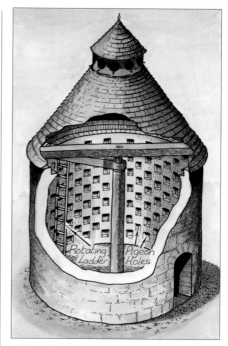

FIG 9.14: *A dovecote, with its distinctive tall form and access for the pigeons in the top.*

house with another delicacy – rabbit – which was introduced by the Normans and bred in purpose-made low banks called warrens.

Churches

Most country houses have a church standing nearby and if the latter building is medieval in origin, then it can indicate that the site has been occupied by a substantial house, in some cases for over a thousand years. It was common for Saxon and Norman nobles to establish a church next to their halls as a status symbol in order to

FIG 9.15: WITLEY COURT, WORCESTERSHIRE: *An 18th-century Classical church, with its distinctive rectangular form, semi-circular arched windows and clock tower with cupola, which had replaced an old decaying medieval structure. The rather plain exterior is in stark contrast to the spectacular white and gold Rococo interior which is one of the finest in the country.*

climb the social ladder. This only fell from fashion in the late 12th century, by which time most medieval parish churches had been established. When villages were later re-sited or fell into decline, the church was left behind next to the house, often receiving a Classical makeover or being completely rebuilt to complement the style of house. The Catholic Emancipation Act of 1829 also meant that suppressed Catholic nobles could pray openly and fashionable Gothic brick churches appeared on some of their estates.

The owner of a large country house would usually have a private chapel. He and his family would only attend the parish church on a Sunday when they would expect a private set of pews and even a fireplace so they did not have to suffer the sermon in discomfort. It was also the practice for the church to hold the family monuments, usually in a side chapel or aisle. Even when the noble decided to move his seat to another of his houses, family burials would still take place in the original parish.

Ice Houses

Ice houses were built to keep large quantities of frozen water available all year round. They were insulated pits covered by a brick dome with an air vent to reduce damp (which accelerated melting), with access through a small tunnel with at least two sets of doors to keep the interior cool. The ice would be collected in winter from a lake, pond or canal by estate workers, using hooks, mallets and rammers. It was then dragged along to the ice house where it would be broken up and compacted in the bottom of the pit with straw laid between for insulation. For the ice to last the whole year, the position and construction of the ice house were critical. For convenience, it was usually sited near the source of the ice and built into a slope so that any melt water could flow out of the bottom. It was often surrounded by trees for shade. As you can imagine, the ice collected off the top of the lake could be pretty mucky and was only used to cool bottles or was placed in ice boxes. Only

FIG 9.16: *A section through a 19th-century ice house. Doors set along the tunnel would lead to the pit in which the ice was held, with an iron or wooden grate at the bottom which allowed any melt water to drain off via the pipe while a sandwich of brick, stone, charcoal and clay insulated the interior. All that may be seen today is the gated entrance to a tunnel set in the side of a mound within a wooded area.*

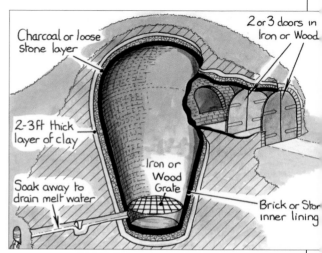

Charcoal or loose stone layer

2-3ft thick layer of clay

Soak away to drain melt water

Iron or Wood Grate

2 or 3 doors in Iron or Wood

Brick or Stone inner lining

imported ice available from the mid 19th century was of good enough quality to be placed directly into drinks.

Gatehouses and Lodges

Gatehouses were built to strengthen the defences of the entrance to a castle and, later, to walled manor houses. By the 15th century, though, they were more for display than for military reasons. A senior member of the lord's household would reside in the room above the gate while a porter controlled entry to the courtyard beyond (as is still the case at many ancient universities and colleges today). The last gatehouses were built in the early 17th century. Afterwards, with the boundary of the park moving further away from the house, a pair of lodges either side of the entry to the main drive became the norm. Classically-styled lodges in the 18th century and quaint Gothic or Italianate cottages in the 19th century usually housed an elderly member of staff who, at the sound of a horn or whistle from an approaching coach, would open the gates.

FIG 9.17: STOKESAY CASTLE, SHROPSHIRE: *A 16th-century, timber-framed gatehouse, with accommodation above for a senior member of staff.*

FIG 9.18: BURTON AGNES HALL, DRIFFIELD, EAST YORKSHIRE: *An early 17th-century gatehouse, with distinctive ogee-shaped caps to the towers and odd proportions to the Classical ornaments above the semi-circular arched opening. The hall behind was built from 1601–10 to a design attributed to Robert Smythson, although next to it the original 12th-century hall can still be visited.*

SECTION III

QUICK
REFERENCE
GUIDE

PLACES TO VISIT

This is a list of the houses featured in the book which are open to the public. Houses maintained by the National Trust are marked (**NT**) and those by English Heritage marked (**EH**). See the Further Information on page 121 for details on visiting these properties.

Baddesley Clinton (NT), Rising Lane, Baddesley Clinton, Knowle, Solihull B93 0DQ Tel. 01564 783294
Fig 7.14
A charming medieval moated manor house, with secret priest holes.

Belton House (NT), Grantham, Lincolnshire NG32 2LS
Tel. 01476 566116
Fig 3.1
A beautiful and largely unaltered late 17th-century house.

Baddesley Clinton

Biddulph Grange Gardens (NT), Biddulph, Stoke on Trent ST8 7SD
Tel. 01782 517999
Figs 5.22, 9.7, 9.9
Notable Victorian gardens restored by the National Trust around an Italianate-style house.

Blackwell, the Arts and Crafts House, Windermere, Cumbria LA23 3JT Tel. 01539 446139; www.blackwell.org.uk
Figs 6.15, 7.1
Outstanding Arts and Crafts interior from the turn of the 20th century.

Blenheim Palace, Woodstock, Oxfordshire OX20 1PX Tel. 08700 602080;
www.blenheimpalace.com
Figs 3.5, 3.9
Designed by John Vanbrugh for the 1st Duke of Marlborough and built between 1705–22. It is one of the finest Baroque mansions in the country.

Blickling Hall (NT), Blickling, Norwich NR11 6NF
Tel. 01263 738030
Figs 2.6, 2.11
An excellent example of an early 17th-century Jacobean house, with a notable long gallery.

Brodsworth Hall (EH), Brodsworth, Doncaster, Yorkshire DN5 7XJ
Tel. 01302 724969
Fig 5.14
A beautifully-restored mid Victorian country house, with gardens replanted to their original form.

Blackwell Arts and Crafts House

Buckingham Palace, London SW1A
1AA Tel. 0207 766 7300;
www.royalcollection.org.uk
Fig 5.2
The original Buckingham House was
rebuilt by John Nash and Edward
Blore from the 1820s and refaced in
1913 to form the famous palace we
see today.

Burghley House, Stamford,
Lincolnshire PE9 3JY
Tel. 01780 752451;
www.burghley.co.uk
Figs 2.2, 2.10
Largely intact, late 16th-century
prodigy house built for Elizabeth's
Lord Treasurer William Cecil, with
18th-century landscaped parkland by
Capability Brown.

Burton Agnes Hall, Driffield,
East Yorkshire YO25 4NB
Tel. 01262 490324;
www.burtonagnes.com
Fig 9.18
An Elizabethan house, with a
notable gatehouse and the original
Norman hall still standing next
to it.

Calke Abbey (NT), Ticknall,
Derbyshire DE73 7LE
Tel. 01332 863822
Fig 7.7
A remarkably untouched, early
18th-century mansion.

Capesthorne Hall, Siddington,
Macclesfield, Cheshire SK11 9JY
Tel. 01625 861221
Fig 5.1
An ancient site, with a house rebuilt in
the Early Victorian period in an early
16th-century style.

Castle Drogo (NT), Drewsteignton,
Exeter EX6 6PB
Tel. 01647 433306
Fig 5.28
An early 20th-century country house,
built in the style of a castle to designs
of Sir Edwin Lutyens.

Castle Howard, Malton, North
Yorkshire YO60 7DA
Tel. 01653 648333;
www.castlehoward.co.uk
Fig 3.4
One of the great country houses
designed by Sir John Vanbrugh
in 1699 and built in the Baroque
style.

Burton Agnes

Chatsworth, Bakewell, Derbyshire, DE45 1PP Tel. 01246 582204; www.chatsworth.org
Fig 3.6
One of the most famous country houses which has been in the Cavendish family for over 450 years and which has developed piecemeal, with notable late 17th- and early 18th-century façades. Edensor village is an excellent example of a relocated village built with picturesque houses in the early Victorian period.

Chiswick House (EH), Burlington Lane, London W4 2RP
Tel. 0207 973 3292
Fig 4.2
Important early Palladian house built from 1725–29 by Lord Burlington.

Cragside (NT), Rothbury, Morpeth, Northumberland NE65 7PX
Tel. 01669 620333
Fig 5.16
Domestic revival house built in the 1870s to designs by Richard Norman Shaw for the inventive Lord Armstrong.

Cronkhill, Attingham Park Estate (NT), Atcham, Shrewsbury SY5 6JP
Tel. 01743 708123
Fig 5.8
An Italianate villa designed by John Nash in 1805 and part of the Attingham Park Estate.

Dunham Massey (NT), Altrincham, Cheshire WA14 4SJ
Tel. 0161 941 1025
Fig 9.12
A house with elements of most periods, which retains its medieval moat and deer park.

Haddon Hall, Bakewell, Derbyshire DE45 1LA Tel. 01629 812855; www.haddonhall.co.uk
Dramatically situated medieval house, with notable long gallery.

Hampton Court Palace, Kingston upon Thames, Surrey KT8 9AU
Tel. 0844 482 7777;
www.hrp.org.uk/HamptonCourtPalace
Fig 1.4 and page 114
Famous palace originally built by Cardinal Wolsey until he fell out of favour with Henry VIII who took it over and extended it, with further work by Wren in the late 17th century.

Hardwick Hall (NT), Doe Lea, Chesterfield, Derbyshire S44 5QJ. Tel. 01246 850430
Fig 2.1
Famous late 16th-century prodigy house built for Bess of Hardwick next to the old hall (managed by English Heritage) which was completed only a few years before she began work on the current building.

Hatfield House, Hatfield, Hertfordshire AL9 5NQ
Tel. 01707 287010;
www.hatfield-house.co.uk
Fig 2.8
A magnificent Jacobean house which has been in the Cecil family for over 400 years.

Highclere Castle, Hampshire RG20 9RN Tel. 01635 253210;
www.highclerecastle.co.uk
Figs 5.3, 9.9
An Early Victorian castle form house, used recently as TV's *Downton Abbey*.

Holkham Hall, Wells-next-the-Sea, Norfolk NR23 1AB
Tel. 01328 710227;
www.holkham.co.uk
Fig 4.3
A classic mid 18th-century, Palladian-style house designed by William Kent, with a spectacular marble hall.

Kedleston Hall (NT), Derby DE22 5JH Tel. 01332 842191
Figs 4.4, 4.5, 7.4
A mid 18th-century Palladian house, with some of the best examples of Robert Adam's work.

Little Moreton Hall (NT), Congleton, Cheshire CW12 4SD
Tel. 01260 272018
Figs 1.1, 7.11, 7.12
Famous timber-framed house dating from the late 15th to 16th century, with notable glazed windows and long gallery.

Longleat, Warminster, Wiltshire BA12 7NW Tel. 01985 844400;
www.longleat.co.uk
Fig 2.5
One of the finest country houses built from the 1560s by Sir John Thynne, with a landscaped park by Capability Brown.

Lowther Castle, Askham, Penrith, Cumbria, CA10 2HG Tel. 01931 712192; www.lowther.co.uk
Fig 5.7
Beautifully set, early 19th-century, castle-style mansion, now just a shell but with the grounds undergoing restoration and open to visitors. Visit the website for details.

Lyme Park (NT), Disley, Stockport, Cheshire SK12 2NX
Tel. 01663 762023
Figs 2.12, 4.1
A 16th-century house, with a graceful, early 18th-century front overlooking the lake.

Nether Winchendon House, nr Aylesbury, Buckinghamshire HP18 0DY Tel. 01844 290101;
www.netherwinchedonhouse.com
Fig 5.5
A house with medieval origins, but

Lyme Park

with a makeover in the late 18th century in the Gothick style.

Powis Castle (NT), Welshpool SY21 8RF   Tel. 01938 551929
Fig 9.3
Medieval castle in origin but notable now for its gardens.

Royal Pavilion, Brighton, East Sussex BN1 1EE Tel. 01273 292746;
www.royalpavilion.org.uk
Fig 5.9
A reworking of an earlier house in an Indian style by John Nash from 1815–23.

Shugborough Hall, Milford, Stafford ST17 0XB Tel. 01889 881388;
www.shugborough.org.uk
Figs 4.6, 5.10, 9.9
A reworking in the Neo Classical style, of an earlier house which is notable today as a working estate, much as it would have been in the 19th century.

Standen (NT), East Grinstead, West Sussex RH19 4NE Tel. 01342 323029
Fig 5.18
One of the few Arts and Crafts houses open to the public, designed by Philip Webb with Morris and Co interiors and demonstrating the movement's ideas of using local materials and retaining original features.

Stanton Harcourt Manor House and Gardens, Main Road, Witney, Oxfordshire OX29 5RJ Tel. 01865 881928
Fig 8.3
Medieval site, with rare kitchen.

Stokesay Castle (EH), Craven Arms, Shropshire, SY7 9AH Tel. 01588 672544
Figs 1.2, 1.8, 9.17
A notable medieval fortified manor house, complete with its original hall, solar, fortifications and later timber-framed gatehouse.

Stowe House, Stowe School, Buckingham MK18 5EH Tel. 01280 818229; www.shpt.org.
Figs 4.18, 9.9, 9.10
A magnificent 18th-century house, with huge marble saloon. The house was sold in 1922 and is now part of the school, while the notable landscaped gardens are managed by the National Trust.

Sudbury Hall (NT), Sudbury, Ashbourne, Derbyshire DE6 5HT Tel. 01283 585305.
Figs 3.2, 3.15
A late 17th-century house, with earlier

Jacobean elements which made it rather outdated when it was built. Notable long gallery and carved staircase.

Sutton Scarsdale Hall (EH), Chesterfield, Derbyshire S44 5UR Tel. 01604 735400 (regional office).
Fig 3.14
The shell of an early Georgian house which was asset stripped in the 1920s. As you are free to wander around, it gives a unique opportunity to see how the structure was built.

Tatton Park (NT), Knutsford, Cheshire WA16 6QN Tel. 01625 374400; www.tattonpark.org.uk
Figs 4.7, 9.8
Neo Classical house, notable for its estate buildings, gardens and parkland.

Tyntesfield (NT), Wraxall, North Somerset BS48 1NT Tel. 01275 461900.
Fig 5.12
An outstanding example of a Gothic Revival country house.

Uppark (NT), South Harting, Petersfield, Hampshire GU31 5QR Tel. 01730 825415
Fig 3.3
An excellent example of a late 17th-century, Dutch-style house.

Waddesdon Manor (NT), Waddesdon, Aylesbury, Buckinghamshitre HP18 0JH Tel. 01296 653211; www.waddesdon.org.uk
Fig 5.15
Spectacular French chateau-style house

built on top of a hill in the 1870s and '80s.

Wightwick Manor (NT), Wightwick Bank, Wolverhampton, West Midlands WV6 8EE Tel. 01902 761400
Figs 5.17, 5.24
Arts and Crafts-style house and interior.

Witley Court (EH), Great Witley, Worcestershire WR6 6JT Tel. 01299 896636.
Figs 4.17, 6.9, 9.11, 9.15
A Jacobean house rebuilt in the early 19th century but now standing as a shell. Notable not only to understand the structure of the house but also for the spectacular fountains and church which have been restored to their former glory.

Wollaton Hall, Nottingham NG8 2AE Tel. 0115 915 3900; www.wollatonhall.org.uk
Figs 2.3, 2.15
Excellent example of a late 16th-century prodigy house, set in parkland close to the city centre.

Wightwick Manor

FURTHER INFORMATION

◈

The largest collection of country houses is in the hands of the National Trust and membership can offer you unparalleled value to access some of the finest pieces of architecture and art in the country. For more information and a guide to visiting their houses visit **www.nationaltrust.org.uk**

A number of other houses and castles are maintained by English Heritage and membership and visiting details can be found on their website **www.english-heritage.org.uk**

For a general guide to visiting country houses I would recommend **Hudson's Historic Houses & Gardens Guide** which is published annually, listing all properties open to the public, including those in private hands. For more information and to purchase the guide, visit **www.hudsonsheritage.com**

There is an immense wealth of information now online about specific houses, their history and visiting them. Just enter the name of the property into your search engine. Here are a few other sites with more general information and links to further sources:

www.buildinghistory.org : Information on all building types.
www.british-history.ac.uk : Information on manors and houses from each county held within the Victoria County History series.
www.stately-homes.com : Gazetteer of properties to visit.
www.dicamillocompanion.com : Brief guides to country houses.
www.lostheritage.org.uk : Fascinating information on demolished country houses.

This book forms just part of a series covering all aspects of period houses from the Tudor age to the 1950s and building histories, including castles and abbeys. Visit **www.countrysidebooks.co.uk** for further information.

Below are listed a few other books which have further information about country houses:

Cruickshank, Dan *The Country House Revealed: A Secret History of the British Ancestral Home*
Girouard, Mark *Life in the English Country House: A Social and Architectural History*
Jenkins, Simon *England's Thousand Best Houses*
Musson, Jeremy and Barker, Paul *English Country House Interiors*
Pevsner, Nikolaus *The Buildings of England series* (yalebooks.co.uk/pevsner.asp)
Sambrook, Pamela A. and Brears, Peter *The Country House Kitchen 1650-1900* (National Trust)

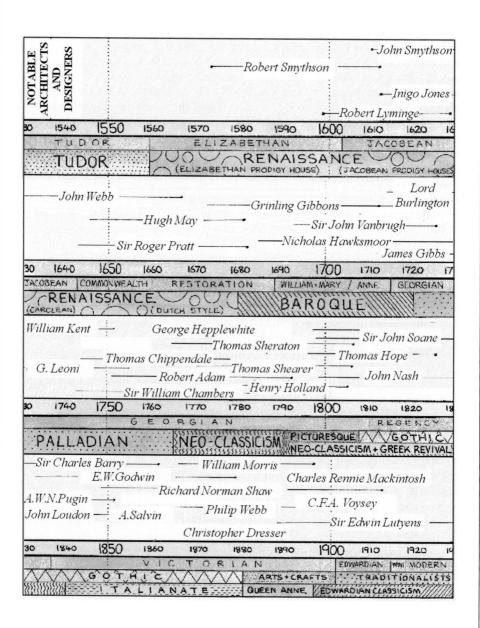

NOTABLE ARCHITECTS AND DESIGNERS

John Smythson
Robert Smythson
Inigo Jones
Robert Lyminge

| 30 | 1540 | 1550 | 1560 | 1570 | 1580 | 1590 | 1600 | 1610 | 1620 | 16 |

TUDOR — ELIZABETHAN — JACOBEAN

TUDOR — RENAISSANCE (ELIZABETHAN PRODIGY HOUSE) (JACOBEAN PRODIGY HOUSES)

John Webb
Hugh May
Sir Roger Pratt
Grinling Gibbons
Sir John Vanbrugh
Nicholas Hawksmoor
Lord Burlington
James Gibbs

| 30 | 1640 | 1650 | 1660 | 1670 | 1680 | 1690 | 1700 | 1710 | 1720 | 17 |

JACOBEAN | COMMONWEALTH | RESTORATION | WILLIAM + MARY / ANNE | GEORGIAN

RENAISSANCE (CAROLEAN) (DUTCH STYLE) — BAROQUE

William Kent
G. Leoni
George Hepplewhite
Thomas Sheraton
Thomas Chippendale
Robert Adam
Sir William Chambers
Thomas Shearer
Henry Holland
Sir John Soane
Thomas Hope
John Nash

| 30 | 1740 | 1750 | 1760 | 1770 | 1780 | 1790 | 1800 | 1810 | 1820 | 18 |

GEORGIAN — REGENCY

PALLADIAN — NEO-CLASSICISM — PICTURESQUE / GOTHIC
NEO-CLASSICISM + GREEK REVIVAL

Sir Charles Barry
E.W.Godwin
A.W.N.Pugin
John Loudon
A.Salvin
William Morris
Richard Norman Shaw
Philip Webb
Christopher Dresser
Charles Rennie Mackintosh
C.F.A. Voysey
Sir Edwin Lutyens

| 30 | 1840 | 1850 | 1860 | 1870 | 1880 | 1890 | 1900 | 1910 | 1920 | 19 |

VICTORIAN | EDWARDIAN | WWI MODERN

GOTHIC — ARTS + CRAFTS — TRADITIONALISTS
ITALIANATE — QUEEN ANNE — EDWARDIAN CLASSICISM

GLOSSARY

abutment: A wall which supports the arch of a bridge or vaulted ceiling.

aisle: A side space running along a hall and separated by a row of posts or columns.

anthemion: A decorative honeysuckle flower.

apse: A semi-circular area at one end of a church or room.

arcade: A row of arches and columns.

architrave: The lowest part of the entablature and the surround of a doorway.

ashlar: Blocks of smooth stone masonry with fine joints.

astylar: A façade with no vertical features like columns.

atrium: A top lit court rising through a number of storeys.

balustrade: A row of decorated uprights (balusters) with a rail along the top.

blind: An arcade, balustrade or portico where the openings are filled in.

bonding: The way bricks are laid in a wall which can be recognised by the pattern made by the headers (short end of a brick) and stretchers (long side of a brick). Two common forms are English bond, with a row of stretchers above a row of headers was popular in the 16th and 17th century, and Flemish bond, with rows of alternate headers and stretchers which largely replaced the English bond by the 18th century.

capital: The decorated top of a column.

cartouche: A usually oval-shaped tablet featuring a coat of arms.

caryatids: Female figures supporting an entablature.

casement: A window which is hinged at the side.

castellated: A battlemented feature.

Coade stone: A form of ceramic stone which was made in the late 18th and early 19th century and named after its original manufacturer Eleanor Coade. The recipe was subsequently lost.

coffered ceiling: A ceiling with sunken panels (coffers).

colonnade: A row of columns supporting an entablature.

cornice: Top section of an entablature which also features around the top of interior and exterior walls.

console: An ornamental bracket with an 'S'-shaped centre.

cupola: A small domed round or polygonal tower which stands on top of a roof or dome.

dormer window: An upright window set in the angle of the roof casting light into an attic room which was usually used for sleeping quarters (from the French verb *dormer* – 'to sleep').

double pile: A house which is two rooms deep.

drip moulding: A moulding running along the top of a window to protect it from rain.

eaves: The roof overhang projecting over a wall.

entablature: The horizontal feature supported by columns.

entasis: A straight-sided column appears to curve inwards so Greeks made them slightly thicker in the middle to counter this effect.

fluting: Vertical concave grooves running up a column or pilaster.

frieze: The middle of the entablature.

gable: The triangular-shaped top of an end wall between the slopes of a roof.

hipped roof: A roof with a slope on all four sides. A gabled roof has two vertical end walls (gables).

jambs: The sides of a door opening.

keystone: The top, centre stone of an arch which can be projected out as a feature.

lantern: A small tower on top of a dome which lets in light to illuminate the interior.

lintel: A flat beam which is fitted above a doorway or window to take the load of the wall above.

loggia: A gallery or corridor open on one side, with a row of columns.

louvre: An opening, usually with slats, through which smoke can escape from a hearth.

mansard roof: A roof with a steep-sided lower section and low pitched top part which creates more room in the attic below.

moulding: A decorative strip in wood, stone or plaster.

mullion: The vertical bars of a window.

oculus: A circular opening, often on a dome or mansard roof.

oratory: A small private chapel.

orders: The different styles of the column and entablature together from Classical architecture.

oriel window: A large projecting window.

parapet: A low wall running along the edge of the roof above the main wall or along the top of a hipped roof on 17th-century, Dutch-style houses.

pediment: A low pitched triangular feature, supported by columns on the top of a portico or Classical doorway.

piano nobile: The floor on which the principal rooms are contained, usually above a raised basement or ground floor.

pilaster: A rectangular column projecting slightly from the wall, with the same treatment at the top and bottom as a free-standing column.

portico: A porch with a flat entablature or triangular pediment supported on columns.

plinth: The projecting base of a wall or the block on which a column stands.

quoins: Dressed stones at the corner of buildings.

rotunda: A circular building with a dome on top.

rustication: The cutting of masonry into blocks separated by deep lines and sometimes with a rough hewn finish. Often used to distinguish the basement of Palladian houses.

sash: A window which slides vertically (a Yorkshire sash slides horizontally).

shaft: The main cylindrical part of a column.

sill: The horizontal beam at the bottom of a window, door or timber-framed wall.

solar: An upper withdrawing room behind the lord's end of a medieval hall.

stucco: A durable smooth plaster coating applied to the outside of houses often over brick in lieu of stone. It was particularly popular in the Regency period.

tracery: The ribs at the top of a stone window which are formed into patterns (usually on churches, chapels, and medieval halls).

transom: The horizontal bars of a window.

tympanum: The flat triangular space within a pediment.

vault: An arched ceiling formed from brick or stone, and sometimes imitated in plaster and wood.

Venetian windows: A window in three vertical sections, the centre one being taller and arched.

voissoir: A wedge-shaped stone which forms an arch.

Other Titles in This Series

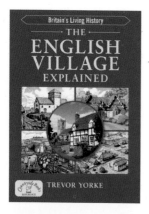

Britain's Living History
THE
ENGLISH
VILLAGE
EXPLAINED

TREVOR YORKE

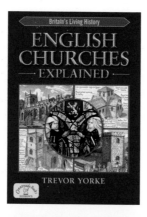

Britain's Living History
ENGLISH
CHURCHES
EXPLAINED

TREVOR YORKE

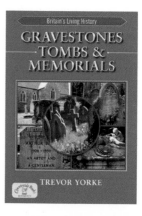

Britain's Living History
GRAVESTONES
TOMBS &
MEMORIALS

TREVOR YORKE

England's Living History
ENGLISH
PLACE-NAMES
EXPLAINED
CHARLES WHYNNE-HAMMOND

England's Living History
PERIOD HOUSE
FIXTURES
&
FITTINGS
1300–1900

LINDA HALL

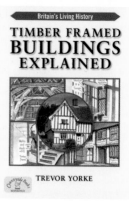

Britain's Living History
TIMBER FRAMED
BUILDINGS
EXPLAINED

TREVOR YORKE

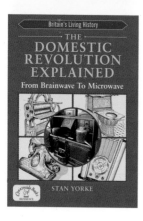

Britain's Living History
THE
DOMESTIC
REVOLUTION
EXPLAINED
From Brainwave To Microwave

STAN YORKE

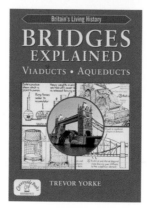

Britain's Living History
BRIDGES
EXPLAINED
VIADUCTS • AQUEDUCTS

TREVOR YORKE

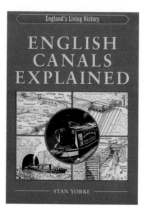

England's Living History
ENGLISH
CANALS
EXPLAINED

STAN YORKE